THE STORY OF A THRONE

THE

STORY OF A THRONE

(CATHERINE II. OF RUSSIA)

FROM THE FRENCH OF

KAZIMIERZ WALISZEWSKI

IN TWO VOLUMES

VOL. II.

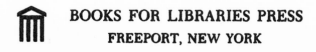

BOOKS FOR LIBRARIES PRESS
FREEPORT, NEW YORK

First Published 1895
Reprinted 1971

INTERNATIONAL STANDARD BOOK NUMBER:
0-8369-5819-5

LIBRARY OF CONGRESS CATALOG CARD NUMBER:
79-157358

PRINTED IN THE UNITED STATES OF AMERICA

CONTENTS

PART II—*THE SEMIRAMIS OF THE NORTH*

PART III—*PRIVATE LIFE.—COURT LIFE*

PART II.

THE SEMIRAMIS OF THE NORTH

CHAPTER II.

MEN OF LETTERS, SCHOLARS, AND ARTISTS.

I.

IN the European kingdom of the mind, which was hers in the estimation of some of the most brilliant subjects that could be found there, and of which she claimed, if not the cares, at all events the honours of sovereignty, Catherine allowed a privileged place to philosophy. Nevertheless, letters, the arts, and even the sciences, had their share of favour. What that share was we shall endeavour to define as exactly as possible.

Catherine had no desire to be the creator of literary, artistic, or scientific glories ; she annexed those already in existence, as she annexed the Polish or the Turkish provinces. She distributed abundant compliments, medals in gold or bronze, more often bronze, and from time to time a little money : to Sedaine for his comedies, to Guys for his *Travels in Greece*, to the Abbé de Saint-Sulpice for his philanthropic establishments, to La Harpe, to Dorat, to Marmontel, to Volney, to the Abbé Galiani. She sent furs to Mademoiselle Clairon, to

Lekain, to Preville, to Bellecour. She bought from Philidor the *Carmen saeculare*, a composition more lauded than loved by the public ; from a Capuchin of the Rue Saint-Honoré, Father Chrysologue, a planisphere of his invention. She was more generous in the purchase of collections, for there she got her money-value in kind ; she offered five hundred thousand livres for the cabinet of Pellerin, the famous numismatologist, who, for his part, preferred to remain *Velche*, and to part with his unrivalled collection to Louis XVI. for less than half the amount. She begged the King to increase Madame d'Épinay's pension. She wrote with her own hand no less than three rough drafts of a complimentary letter to Marmontel, and she sent with it a printed translation of his *Bélisaire*, in which the Orlofs, the Shuvalofs, and the Tshernishofs had collaborated with her. All this gained for her an absolute servility of homage, and all but a deification in praise.

The richest tribute of both the one and the other came from France, which indeed was the main recipient of the petty favours of Semiramis. " If your august ancestor has deserved immortality in Russia, it is in France that she has obtained it," said Suard to the Emperor Alexander in 1824, and it was the absolute truth. La Harpe and Dorat wrote rhymed epistles in honour of the great Catherine on the model of those addressed by Boileau to Louis the Great ; Thomas devoted the last years of his life to the glorification, in a very indifferent *Pétréide*, of the heiress and the successor of Peter I. Volney, who was then writing his *Considérations sur la guerre des Turcs avec les Russes,* endeavoured to justify the political system adopted by the Empress in the East. In his *Tableau de Paris,* Mercier proposed as an example to the Dauphin the conduct of the great Empress ; not her private conduct, doubtless. Even the Church ranged itself on her side, though the St. Catherine of Voltaire scarcely seems, at first sight, to possess the qualities requisite to figure in its calendar. Her officiants waved the censer before her with the greatest zeal, from the Abbé Gaubert, the obscure writer of a dull poem which drew from her a medal, and the Abbé Roman, writer of a poem on *Inoculation,* dedicated to the sovereign, to the Abbé de Lubersac, who seized the opportunity of the visits paid by the Grand-Duke Paul to the establishments at Paris, in 1782, to instruct his readers concerning those of St. Petersburg, which he confidently imagined were at least as fine, if not finer.

Thus fervently preached and practised, the cult of St. Catherine found but few recalcitrants : Mably making certain reservations in regard to the policy of the Empress in Poland ; Raynal describing the famous legislative assembly at Moscow as a farce ; Rousseau getting out of the way of the advances which came to him from this quarter, more perhaps from force of habit than from conviction. In the feminine clan, a certain coldness manifested itself, even certain definite individual revolts : even the imperial "fag" in person could not arouse the devotion of Mademoiselle de Lespinasse. "Grimm is back again," she wrote to the Abbé Galiani. "I have overwhelmed him with questions ; he represents

the Tsarina not as a sovereign, but as an amiable
woman, full of wit, of vivacity, of everything that can
attract and charm.   In all that he told me I seemed
to see rather the captivating art of a Greek courtesan
than the dignity and lustre of the Empress of a great
empire."   Madame du Deffant was very sceptical on
the subject, and, in writing to her, her "grandmother,"
the Duchesse de Choiseul, abandoned herself to a wordy
and violent diatribe on the relations of Semiramis with
Voltaire.   In 1794 Madame de Staël, writing to Meister,
the friend and collaborator of Grimm, in reference to a
conspiracy, abetted by Catherine, against the regent
of Sweden, said : " Your Empress has done us much
harm.   They say that she even knows of my existence.
I wish I could forget hers ! "

There were also certain dissidents, fervent in their
way, but forming a church of their own.   Figuring as
he did in 1770 among the most ardent devotees of the
faith according to Catherine, the Abbé Galiani refused
to admit all its dogmas, as formulated by the High
Priest of Ferney.   That of tolerance, for instance, inscribed on the Voltairian *credo* among the virtues exercised by St. Catherine, he could not accept.   As he
confessed to D'Alembert : " *His* Catherine is a great
woman, because she is intolerant and triumphs, and
all great men have been, and must be, intolerant."   It
is true that he sometimes amused himself by signing
his letters *Machiavellini*, and his schism did not prevent
him from joining with Diderot in a project for an inscription to be placed on the base of the statue of
Peter the Great, by which the work of Falconet was

to be transformed into a monument to the glory of
Catherine. He attempted a Latin epigram:

> " *Catharina II. Augusta*
> *Mater senatus, Mater castrorum*
> *Mater Patriae,*" *etc.*

Catherine was better inspired in her own interests,
and wrote simply:

> " *Petro primo*
> *Catharina secunda.*"

But she bought from the Abbé a cabinet of books
and prints, collected by his brother, Bernard, the labori-
ous editor of Vitruvius, taking it from him at his own
price. Later on he had a little difficulty with her in
regard to a medal for which he was kept waiting a
long time. But the imperial " fag " had to suffer
for it. " Monster of forgetfulness," wrote the Abbé,
" what do you mean by all the teasing and tantalizing
hopes that you held out to me? Do you not see that
my bad luck is so momentous that it changes the order
and nature of the universe? Is it in nature that a
sovereign who has poured out millions in presents, who
scatters them as the sun does his rays upon the just
and the unjust, should hesitate for three or four years
before making up her mind to send you a bronze medal
for me? I rage against my incredible fate." But the
medal came at last, and Grimm no doubt handed on
the passage in the Empress's letter alluding to it:
" What is there so very extraordinary if he should be
on the reverse of a medal? Has no one ever seen a
genius before? " The Abbé at once ceased to lament

against his fate. He made his will, in which he stated that the famous sword that had belonged to the Duc de Valentinois was to be offered for three hundred ducats to a collector who had manifested the desire to possess it, and that if he refused the terms, it was to be respectfully offered to the Empress of Russia, " in souvenir of infinite gratitude for all her kindnesses."

Rulhière, who never received a medal, not even a bronze medal, made a very different sort of sacrifice on behalf of the Empress. In the preface to the first edition of his *History of the Revolution in Russia*, not published till 1797, after his death and that of Catherine, the delay in the appearance of the work is set down to a pledge of honour given by the author, after having refused a sum of thirty thousand livres, offered by the Empress for some corrections and suppressions to which he declined to consent. We are left in doubt as to the reasons which could have induced him to consent, in default of this concession, to an arrangement which seems much more to Catherine's advantage ; and Diderot, who acted as mediator, and corresponded on the subject with Falconet, gives us no further explanation. " The Empress's librarian " was one of the first to advise the suppression of the work, though the author had represented the sovereign, " our sovereign," he wrote to Falconet, " as a great woman, *un gran cervello di principessa.*" Catherine wished to see for herself ; but the author refused to give up his MS, or to send her a copy ; he pretended that he had never had any idea of publishing the book, but had composed it merely to satisfy the curiosity of a few friends. She was none the less anxious. The friends thus privileged were fairly numerous: D'Alembert read the MS, after the Comtesse d'Egmont, and also Madame Geoffrin, and many others. And they all gave the most reassuring accounts of it, D'Alembert declaring that he preferred the truth as it was presented by Rulhière to all the apologies, and the Duc de la Rochefoucault declaring that he had found it not indeed " a notable confession," but "a notable life " ; Diderot finally summing up the matter thus : " If you are very anxious, Madame, to have a good reputation for the conventional virtues, the worn-out rags of your sex, then the work is a satire against you ; but if wide views, virile and patriotic ideas, are more your concern, then the author represents you as a great princess, and, taken all in all, he does you more honour than dishonour."

Catherine had reasons of her own for being suspicious. It was not only over her own reputation that she kept watch. She knew by the example of the Abbé Chappe how a Frenchman could speak of Russia and the Russians, after having lived for some time in their midst. She knew too, perhaps, what were likely to be the impressions of the former secretary to the Embassy. Her " black cabinet " did not exist for nothing, and some letters of Rulhière sent from St. Petersburg to Rousseau might have revealed to her phrases of this sort :

" Your treatise on education has not yet found its way to Russia ; these people, who pride themselves, in addition to all their other ambitions, on being amateurs of letters and philosophy, have only got, as far as libraries and printing establishments are concerned, the mere wreck and ruin of those founded by Peter I."

Or again :

" What you say of the Russians is strikingly true . . . The distinctive character of this nation is its genius, or more generally its talent, for imitation. All the Russians, in their little way, possess what their Tsar had in his great way ; they are regular apes, and their native gift would doubtless have caused them to make rapid progress in the arts, if it were not counter-balanced by their vanity, another not less characteristic national defect."

Diderot recommended Catherine to arrange matters by giving Rulhière a place as consul at St. Petersburg. But her relations with Voltaire had given her certain fixed ideas as to the way in which matters of this kind should be arranged with men of letters. She sent her representative at Paris the order to buy the MS. Unluckily, Prince Galitzin, an amiable man, in good repute in literary circles, was not at his post. It was Hotinski, a *chargé d'affaires*, who undertook the arrangement. The result was unfortunate : Rulhière sent the Empress's messenger about his business. Perhaps he had not used due ceremony. That was Diderot's view of the case. " Money is accepted or refused according to the people who offer it," he remarked sententiously. He then undertook the affair himself, and succeeded better. That was in 1768. Five years later, when Diderot was at St. Petersburg, Catherine still questioned him in regard to the terrible MS, which had been put under lock and key, but which always caused her some

anxiety. She died without ever seeing it. Thirty
years later, after the book had been published, Princess
Dashkof declared that it must be a forgery. No Russian translation has appeared to this day, though M.
Longuinof has made one. We have related elsewhere
how Catherine endeavoured to obviate the damage done
to her reputation and that of Russia by the wretched
Abbé whose name we have mentioned above, and who
was far from resembling the Abbé de Lubersac.

The ill-success of Chappe d'Auteroche, as of Rulhière,
in his relations with the empire and the Empress of the
North, was due to his not having followed the advice
given by Madame du Deffant to Voltaire, and to have
challenged that test of personal contact which none
of the literary, artistic, or scientific relations entered
upon by Catherine with Western Europe were able to
survive. In 1766 Semiramis is fired with enthusiasm
for the future author of *L'Ordre naturel et essentiel des
Sociétés politiques*, known then merely for some articles
published in the *Journal de l'Agriculture, du Commerce
et des Finances*. A memorandum drawn up for her
benefit, a recommendation on the part of Diderot, give
her an intense desire to see the author, and even to have
him in her service. What are her intentions in regard
to him? Apparently, if we are to judge by the subsequent course of events, they are extremely indefinite.
But she is excited by the extravagant tirades which the
enthusiastic Diderot does not fail to send to Falconet
in praise of his *protégé's* merits: "Ah! my friend, if
Her Majesty is really devoted to truth, what a treat for
her! I realize and partake in it in advance. We give

up this man for you ; he gives us up for her. . . . When
the Empress has this man, what will be the good of the
Quesnays, the Mirabeaus, the Voltaires, the D'Alemberts,
the Diderots? None, my friend, none! Here is the
man to console her for the loss of Montesquieu." She
must have this man. She is afraid that, having been
for a long time in the diplomatic service at Martinique,
the French Government may hinder him from coming
over to her. She puts the arrangement of affairs into
the hands of Panin.

As for Mercier de la Rivière, he really believes himself
called upon to take in hand the government, at all
events of the home affairs of the empire of the North.
His first concern, on arriving at St. Petersburg, is to
arrange his rooms as offices of the various departments
which he is prepared to direct. The Empress being
absent, he waits upon Count Panin, who promises a
post with a salary of three hundred roubles a month.
The poor Mercier has a more serious fall from the
heights than even Diderot had had, and the following
dialogue ensues between him and the prime minister of
Catherine :

"I had a much higher salary in the King's service.
I can only accept what you offer me as a little addition
to my travelling expenses. And I do not even know
yet in what way I can be of use to Her Majesty."

"You can stay in Russia, and take a place in the
magistracy. Are you not discontented with your court,
and particularly with M. de Choiseul ? "

"I ? Not in the least! The King shows me the
utmost favour, and M. de Choiseul has always been the

best of friends to me. I have so little intention of leaving France for good, that I have put aside my travelling expenses, and have taken leave of absence for two years only. To show you how much this is the case, I have now only to return at once to my own country."

"If that is so, go then; but the Empress will be glad if you will wait at least until she returns to St. Petersburg."

Mercier waited, but to little purpose. A *résumé* which he made for the Empress on his great work on *L'Ordre naturel*, and a new paper on the labours of the Economic Society of St. Petersburg, were not after all enough to induce Catherine to confide to him the administration of her empire. Some tactless proceedings on the part of the man who was to fill the place of Montesquieu added to the Empress's dissatisfaction with him. Besides a numerous following, he had brought from Paris his wife and another lady friend, to whom Madame Mercier seemed to have no objection. These ladies were anxious to enjoy themselves at St. Petersburg, and were soon the subject of much talk. Then, too, when the publicist was in the presence of the Tsarina, he had no idea how to adopt the tone suitable to his station and to his ambitions. "If ever you recommend any one to the Empress," wrote Falconet to Diderot, "see that he keeps the right sort of company. . . If he is admitted to the Empress's circle he should not say, loud enough to be heard, 'A man like me,' for those present will never take that for modesty. When he is arguing about his *Ordre naturel*,

he should not lose his temper with his opponent, and
say : 'You must be very stupid if you don't understand
me.'" Thiébaut records a fragment of conversation with
the Empress herself, who is questioning her guest on his
ideas in regard to legislation :

" God has left it to no man to establish laws."

" In what then consists the science of the legislator ? "

" In the recognition of natural laws."

" I wish you good-day."

The final *congé* soon follows, and Catherine writes
to Grimm, telling him of her disillusion : " Diderot and
Galitzin, and you and Panin and I, have all been on
the wrong scent. We were all blind, we took it all
on trust, from letters, on the authority of twenty people,
but it was very foolish of us ! " She kept a grudge for
a long time against M. Solon la Rivière, as she called
him, and in 1774 she wrote to Voltaire : " M. de la
Rivière, who imagined that six years ago we were
walking on all-fours, and who really took the trouble to
come from Martinique to set us up on our hind legs,
was a little bit out of date."

Nevertheless she began the same thing over again
with Senac de Meilhan. This time it was in connection
with some historical work, on which it was again impossible to come to an agreement. A refugee of the
Revolution, living very quietly at Venice, but calling
himself *Maître de requêtes honoraires et intendant des
provinces de Hainaut et de Cambresis*, Senac suggests
in 1791 that he should write the history of Catherine.
As a specimen of his competence for the task, he sends
an Introduction to the work, which seems attractive, to

the favourite of the moment, Zubof. Catherine, however, instructs her minister at Venice, Mordvinof, to
examine the candidate : " Is he sufficiently *pliable ?* "
The examiner sends in a favourable report. An invitation is at once sent to the future historiographer, and
two thousand ducats are sent him for his travelling
expenses. But it is no longer the history of Catherine
that he is to write : it is to be the history of Russia in
the eighteenth century, not without giving a prominent
place to the reigning Empress. Scarcely has he arrived
at St. Petersburg when the reigning Empress has again
changed her mind : she does not wish to be mentioned
in a historical work published in her lifetime. He must
wait till after her death. But, all the same, she writes
endless letters to the historian, giving a quantity of
suggestions for the work which she asks him not to set
about, including even the materials for a very detailed
portrait of her person.

This foolery goes on for some time, the work remaining in suspense, but Catherine seeming enchanted with
the workman. Suddenly there is a change of front.
In June, in conversation with Grimm, Catherine was
still on the chapter of the charms of *her historian*,
as she called him ; in September, she writes to the
" fag " : " As for M. de Meilhan, who is in very indifferent health, I find in him infinitely more will than
power to do. He has said very little, in the most
charming way. The history, if it is ever done, and I
hope not, will come to the same thing . . . In the
archives at Moscow, the scholars who are there are
scandalized at his frivolity . . . He appears to have

said that in Russia one sees nothing but beards and orders . . . You shall know one day why I sent for M. de Meilhan ; but I found him not up to the work . . . The man is working with all his might, trying to write the history of a country of which he does not know the language."

She complains that the unfortunate Senac has been much too ambitious, that he has wanted to become Minister of the Exchequer, and that he has gone to the army and insisted on giving advice to Patiomkin, "who yawned at it"; that he has even wanted to be appointed ambassador at Constantinople, because he is fond of sofas and the Turkish way of living. She even accuses him of getting into bad repute at St. Petersburg by paying attention to a certain Madame Shtcherbinin, "whose conduct is too bad for anything."

On his side, he discovers, after he has been three months at Moscow, that Russia "is not a bit French," and is greatly disgusted at finding it so. " I should not at all wish it to be so," replies Catherine, to whom he makes the remark. He too writes to her voluminous letters, to one of which she replies : " I see quite well that we shall make whole volumes, and when we have made them, we shall not be any nearer understanding one another than we are now." He takes the hint, and demands leave of absence, asking only for the title of " Intendant of Her Majesty's library." He apparently loves honorary appointments, and collects titles. With a somewhat malicious wit, she points out to him that the equality now established in his country does not admit of distinctions of this kind. Finally, he obtains a pension of fifteen hundred roubles, and goes to Vienna, where, in 1792, he tries to indoctrinate old Prince Kaunitz, and to prove to him that "in a country where everything, ideas included, is topsy-turvy, it is easy to please everybody"; he dies there in 1803.

II.

On the whole, however, the foreign littérateurs and scientists are better treated by Semiramis than those of her own subjects who attempt to follow, timidly and from afar, the course of La Harpe and Dorat, of Mercier and Senac. These last, it is true, have their reasons for not being over-particular. We learn from a note added to the 1740 edition of the works of Tre-diakovski, the poet who charmed the court of Anne, that he had the honour of reciting one of the poems contained in the volume in the presence of the Empress herself. He did it on his knees, by the side of the fire-place, and received as his reward a box on the ears from Her Majesty's own hand.

Catherine does not distribute blows to Trediakovski's later rivals, but, apart from André Shuvalof, who is allowed the honour of re-touching Her Majesty's French correspondence, she admits none of them to her inti-macy. It would be indeed to run even greater risk than with Diderot himself. The memoirs of Timkovski form a picture of these Russian men of letters, including some of the most illustrious of them, Lomonossof and

Sumarokof, for instance, meeting together at the house of John Shuvalof, and spending their time in violent quarrels, accompanied by vollies of the grossest abuse. They call one another drunkards and thieves, and usually end by coming to blows, upon which Shuvalof turns them all out of doors. Sumarokof is the most violent. Having had a quarrel, in 1770, with Belmontia, who plays the principal parts in the Moscow theatre, he rushes upon the stage one day in the midst of the performance, picks up the actress in his arms, and carries her off into the wings, because he has forbidden her to appear in any of his plays. Catherine is very indulgent in regard to the national poet; and she sends this charming reply to the violent and hardly respectful letters in which he attempts to justify his conduct:

"Monsieur Sumarokof! I have been much surprised by your letter of January 28, and still more by that of February 1. Both seemed to be filled with complaints against Belmontia, who has only followed the orders of Count Saltykof. The field-marshal was anxious to see your tragedy, which was a compliment to you. It would have been only seemly in you to have conformed to the desire of the chief person in authority at Moscow . . . I think you know better than any one how much respect is due to those who have served their country with glory, and whose heads have grown white in its service. This is why I advise you to avoid similar disputes in the future. In this way you will preserve the peace of mind which you require for your work, and I shall always prefer to see the passions represented in your plays rather than to read them in your letters."

Before being appointed minister under Alexander I., and not minister of education, but of justice, the poet Dierjavin plays at the court of Catherine, or rather at that of Plato Zubof, a part beside which that of Trediakovski, in the palace of the Empress Anne, seems quite dignified. In its rapid evolution at the rear of the other European nations, Russia at this time begins to run ahead of them in certain moral, even material matters, with a scarcely enviable celerity, and the singer of *Felitsa*, as the friend of persons in high position, figures already as an expert trafficker in occult influences, an eighteenth-century *chéquard* before his time, whom his nineteenth-century rivals might look upon as a master. It is true that the poet does not know himself. His rank in the hierarchy of the *tchin* seems to concern him much more than his place in the temple of the Muses. In praising Catherine in *Felitsa* for not frequenting the too sublime sanctuary, he seems almost to be apologizing for visiting it himself. He compares poetry to "a glass of lemonade, good to take when one is too hot." His artistic education is null. His instinct alone guides him, and at times it guides him well, as in the *Vodopad* (The Cascade), composed on the occasion of the death of Patiomkin, an admirable poem, which almost permits us to pardon him for his ingratitude towards his former protector. On the whole, however, Pushkin has found the exact word in saying that his poems are like "the bad translation of a masterpiece."

Apart from Sumarokof and Dierjavin, the current
of foreign influence, uninterrupted since Elizabeth, in
spite of the nationalist tendencies of the new school, and
stimulated by the apparent preferences of Catherine,
forms around her a whole group of writers, even of
poets, who attempt an even more direct imitation of
Western models than that attempted by Lomonossof,
to the extent even of disdaining their own language,
and rhyming French verses which Voltaire affected to
consider as good as his. Catherine is more reserved
in this respect. The translator of Marmontel seems to
think but little of the lyric gifts of Prince Bielossielski,
whose French works are nevertheless edited by Marmontel himself, and who ends one of his epistles addressed to France, to England, and to the Republicans
of Saint-Marin by this challenge :

> " Réponse, s'il vous plaît !
> Mon adresse en Europe est Apollon cadet."

Was Semiramis very far wrong ?   D'Allonville, referring to this poet in his memoirs, quotes some fragments,
in very dubious taste, from a Pindaric ode to Princess
Dolgoruki, for instance, in which we find verses of this
kind :

> " Je confie aux échos de la machine ronde
> Que rien n'est comparable aux tendres abatis
> De la princesse Pudibonde ; "

or again :

> " Hélas ! serait-il vrai, Pudibonde charmante,
> Que ta belle maman, pour arrondir ce cou,
> T'a claqué d'une main savante,
> T'a claqué doucement je ne saurais dire où ? "

An operetta, which he puts on the stage at St. Petersburg under the name of *Olenka*, puts to flight the spectators, at once bored and disgusted ; and Madame Vigée-Lebrun gives an amusing account of her visit to the prince-poet's picture-gallery :

" What have you come to admire, madame ? "

" Your pictures, Prince."

" I have such a lot.   What school ? "

" The Roman school."

" It has such a lot of painters.   Which would you like to see ? "

" Raphael."

" Madame, Raphael had three manners.   Which would you like to see first ? "

" The third."

" Good."

And this masterpiece of Raphael's third manner turns out to be a shocking daub.

In default of other merits, Bielossielski has at least the merit of being the father of the charming Princess Zenaïde Volkonski, so adored by poets, and so justly. It is true that she may have inherited some of her qualities from her mother's father, a man of rare intelligence and of solid worth, though in a humble capacity : Kozitski, Catherine's favourite secretary.

André Shuvalof, who is not to be confounded, as he generally is, even in Russia, with his uncle John, owes his favour in the eyes of Catherine to his relations with the patriarch of Ferney, his value as an assistant in the French tongue, and his discretion.   His talents as a versifier seem, in spite of the *Épître à Ninon*, to count

for nothing. The *Épître à Ninon* was persistently attributed to Voltaire himself, who not less persistently
denied its authorship, sending to the author, by way of
compliment, this only half-complimentary quatrain :

> " L'Amour, Epicure, Apollon
> Ont dicté vos vers que j'adore ;
> Mes yeux ont vu mourir Ninon,
> Mais Chapelle respire encore."

At the same time, writing to the Duc de Richelieu, he
speaks of a young Russian "who writes French verse
better than all his Académie."

Published in 1774, sixty-eight years after the death of
the famous courtesan, the *Épître à Ninon* had no very
great success in Russia, where too little was known of
the life and glory of the immortal priestess of love,
whose favours were solicited by the Cardinal de Richelieu, and who was protected by Madame de Maintenon.
But every one at St. Petersburg knew the lines to
Nathalie Zagriajska, a beauty with whom the conqueror
of the Taurida was for a moment in love :

> " Cet invincible amour que je porte en mon sein,
> Dont je ne parle pas, mais que tout vous atteste,
> Est un sentiment pur, une flamme céleste
> Que je nourris toujours, hélas ! mais c'est en vain.
> De la séduction je ne suis pas l'apôtre :
> Je serais fortuné possédant vos appas,
> Je vivrai malheureux si vous ne m'aimez pas,
> Je mourrai de douleur si vous aimez un autre."

Neledinski, the Russian translator of *Zaïre*, the
Russian Petrarch, as some of his biographers are audacious enough to call him, thought a good deal of this
fragment. Catherine did not appear to share in the

general enthusiasm. She had the good sense to see, however vaguely, that these Russian versifiers in French were only doing harm to the national poetry and to themselves. But, like his uncle John, whose letters have been attributed to him in every edition of the correspondence of Voltaire, André Shuvalof was in constant intercourse with the great man. He too was set down as a " pupil " of the incomparable master. The honour of having formed this disciple belonged more legitimately, however, to a more modest professor, Pierre Louis de Roy, author of a collection of *Poésies Diverses*, published at Amsterdam in 1757, who was a tutor in Shuvalof's house. Both uncle and nephew were on several occasions guests at Ferney. In 1695, Voltaire gave a performance of *Mérope* and *Nanine* at his theatre in honour of Count André and his young wife, and the latter presented two hundred thousand écus' worth of diamonds to Madame Denis for the performance, and a similar amount to the Marquise de Florian for having played the part of the Baroness in *Nanine*. Shuvalof himself played Égiste in *Mérope*. All this could not fail to give him a certain lustre in the eyes of the Semiramis of the North and her court. It also called forth various rivals. In the year when the *Épître à Ninon* was published, Voltaire referred to one of these in a letter to D'Alembert: "A son of Count Rumiantsof has just been writing French verses, some of which are even more amazing than those of Count Shuvalof. It is a dialogue between God and the Reverend Father Hayer, author of the *Journal Chrétien*. God recommends tolerance to him ; Hayer replies :

' Ciel ! que viens-je d'entendre ? Ah ! ah ! je le vois bien,
   Que vous-même, Seigneur, vous ne valez rien.' "

Even more intimately associated with the intellectual
life of the West, Prince Dimitri Galitzin, Russian
minister, first at Paris, then at the Hague, where he
edited a complete edition of the works of Helvétius,
had at least the wisdom to attempt the French language
only in prose, and only in dealing with scientific subjects.   Catherine, however, did not welcome his efforts
or summon him to the court, for which he was probably
by no means sorry.   Perhaps too she would not have
cared to see at the court the Princess Galitzin, a
daughter of the Prussian general, Schmettau, and one of
the most notable women of the time, alike for her
beauty, her intelligence, and her taste for intrigue.

III.

There are very pretty stories, which one reads in the
French papers, about Catherine's relations with the
artistic world; how the Semiramis of the North took her
ermine mantle off her own shoulders and put it over
Païsiello, who was cold ; replying to her *maître de cour*,
when he brings a complaint against the maestro, like
Napoleon to the prefect who had been ill-treated by
General Lassalle, that she could make fifty *maîtres de
cour* whenever she liked, but not one Païsiello.   It is
pretty, but it is not true.   We shall endeavour to show
what the facts really were.

Catherine never had about her, in actual residence,

any writer or scientist of the first order; for Diderot may be said to have merely paid her court a passing visit. One artist at least, among the greatest of his day, did indeed live there for twelve years ; and unfortunately it is in regard to him that Semiramis acted most unfairly, and failed most signally in the part which has been attributed to her by her admirers, and which she seems indeed to have had some pretensions to play in the world of art. If the career of Falconet, a man of incontestable genius, has never received its due reward in Russia, if his existence there has added some further pages to the martyrology of great men misunderstood, Catherine alone is responsible for it in the eyes of posterity. It was not Russia which was in fault. On the contrary, we may say that the artist owes to Russia the better part of his glory, and the opportunity, if not of absolutely achieving himself, at all events of showing what he might have done had circumstances been more favourable ; if, for example, he had not been forced to begin his career in the workshop of a wig-maker.

When Diderot arrived at St. Petersburg, and went to see his friend, he met with a surprise which he has expressed with his usual frankness and vivacity. It was not that he now first discovered the merit of the sculptor: that he had been among the first to admire and praise. But in the artist of the Pygmalion, and even in the more virile craftsman of the Milo of Crotona, and the *Christ agonisant* of the church of Saint-Roch, it had been especially certain fine and delicate qualities that he had appreciated. The colossal statue of Peter the Great, the model of which he now saw, revealed a quite new force in the artist. " I have seen it, I have indeed seen it," he wrote to the artist, " and I give up passing an opinion on any piece of sculpture, if you have not made a sublime monument. . . . I knew how skilful you were, but may I perish if I ever thought you could do anything like that. You have achieved in your lifetime both a charming idyll and a large piece out of an epic poem." Hyperbolical in his praise as Diderot always was, his appreciation has been contested by modern critics, to whom the work of Falconet seems destitute of individual inspiration, made up of reminiscences and imitations: there is no more improvising at the age of fifty ! Nevertheless the grandeur, the epic touch, that Diderot was not the only one to see at the time, still impresses visitors from the West. And to bring this new quality into the artist's manner, scarcely vivified as yet, idyllic, as Diderot said, is incontestably the doing of Russia, of those large horizons which environ the figure of the great creator, of that creation itself, impressing its own immensity upon the sculptor, its immensity and its savage vigour. As for Catherine, all she did was to torment the poor artist, or to let him be tormented, with a crowd of petty annoyances, and little, irritating pin-pricks.

Art always has been, and still is, more or less down to the present day, a foreign import in Russia. Towards the middle of the fifteenth century the European influence, slowly ousting the Asiatic yoke, replaces, at the court of Ivan III., the Byzantine by the Italian artists. Poland, where Bona Sforza, wife of Sigismund I., attracts a great number of her compatriots, passes on certain of them to her neighbour of Moscow, and they are employed in the construction of the palaces and churches of the Kremlin. After the Italians come the Germans. The turn of France does not come till 1741, the time of Elizabeth, or rather of John Shuvalof, the all-powerful favourite, and the first to set on foot the anti-Germanic movement. Rastrelli is indeed, in 1761, the architect of the Winter Palace, but it is Lamothe who, in 1767, directs the building of the Hermitage; he is followed by Valois at St. Petersburg, and with Lorrain then Lagrenée, Doyen, and Houdon, French art is soon out of all rivalry. Ere long, measures have to be taken in France in order to put a stop to the emigration of French artists, attracted by the favours held out to them on the banks of the Neva. In 1767 a certain Daniel Barral is arrested at Strasburg on a charge of unlawfully tampering with French artists on behalf of Russia.

The idea of a statue of Peter the Great had already haunted the brain of Elizabeth. But Rastrelli dies before he has carried the work to completion, and Martelli, who succeeds him, is interrupted in turn by the death of the Empress. When he has finished his sketch, Catherine is on the throne, and she is not satisfied by the conventional hero in Greek costume who is presented to her. She dreams of something quite different, she knows not what, and she looks to Paris for some one who can give form to this vague dream. Her appeal to Falconet in 1766 is however a mere chance; or rather it is the modesty and disinterestedness of the sculptor which decide it, rather than a real appreciation of his artistic skill. It is a cheap bargain, and that decides

Semiramis. The other French artists ask four hundred
and fifty thousand livres at the very lowest for undertaking the journey and carrying out the work. Falconet,
to whom three hundred thousand livres are offered,
strikes off a third of the price himself. It is characteristic of the man who, having undertaken in 1747 to
execute, after a design of Coypel, a symbolic group,
" France embracing the bust of the King," took fifteen
years to carry out this official order, and, having sent it
in at last, begged to be allowed to destroy it, " one of
the worst," he said, " that could be done in sculpture,"
offering to return the nine thousand livres that he had
received for his work.

The Empress is at Moscow when he arrives at St.
Petersburg. This is very much in his favour. A correspondence at once begins between Empress and artist,
soon dropping into that tone of familiarity which Catherine was always ready to adopt in such relations. From
October 1766 to January 1768, the date of the Empress's
return, the frequent exchange of often very long letters
goes on uninterruptedly, and, as usual, Catherine at first
finds it very charming. " His letters are really original,"
she writes to Grimm, " or those of an original, and you
know that we do not dislike that." But it is an impression which does not last. Nothing lasts, indeed, with
this woman whose genius is so variable, *ondoyant et
divers*, and in this too so feminine. By the time she
returns to St. Petersburg she has already cooled down
in regard to the artist, and even in regard to the work
with which she has entrusted him. She does not visit
his studio for six weeks,

He, however, has set about his task with immense ardour. He meets with unexpected difficulties; he finds himself surrounded with persons who, while they might say with Catherine that they have no opinion in regard to sculpture, as they have never had the opportunity of seeing a statue, all the same insist on giving the artist advice as to what he is to do. Betzki, the most enlightened of the lot, one day suggests that Peter the Great should be made to look in a different direction with each eye, at the Admiralty with one, and with the other at the twelve "colleges" of the empire, contained in a very ugly building opposite. Catherine happily does not countenance this wild notion : but she does not use her authority to put a stop to the bickerings, indiscretions, and even insults, to which the sculptor is daily exposed. Betzki one day has the idea that the artist should undertake a statue of Catherine at the same time as that of Peter the Great. Falconet, almost immediately afterwards, shows him a model in clay for the monument.

" How much ? " queries Betzki.

" Nothing. That is enough for me in itself."

" You are very clever, but we know what generosity of that sort means ; it comes too dear."

" You shall see how clever I am ! "

And the sculptor seizes his model, and breaks it to pieces.

Perhaps he is too quick-tempered and too sensitive. That is the opinion of Diderot himself, who calls him "the Jean Jacques of sculpture," and writes to him : " You are too ready to believe anything unfavourable ;

your sensitiveness carries you too far ; one evil-minded person could put you at loggerheads with a whole city." Falconet announces to his friend "that he has become more bearish than ever," and Diderot replies : "That is impossible." Catherine too advises him not to pay so much heed to tattlers. Surly as he is, he is not without wit, and one day he translates the usual inscription *Vache Vysokorodie* (Your High Birth) which he finds on a letter to Catherine, remarking : "That would suit me admirably, for I was born in an attic." But he is brought into considerable straits. On his arrival he has once more shown his disinterestedness : on being offered three thousand five hundred roubles for his maintenance, he contents himself with taking half. At the end of six years he finds that provisions have gone up in price, and that he is unable to make both ends meet. Thereupon he demands a few hundred roubles extra. A sort of inspector of the Beaux-Arts, who calls himself Lascaris, and who is an adventurer of the deepest dye, replies that "he has already cost too much." " M. Lascaris apparently takes me for the big stone," writes the poor artist to Catherine, alluding to the vast expense which has been occasioned by the transport to St. Petersburg of the great mass of rock on which the bronze equestrian statue is to be erected. Not long after, he himself intercedes in favour of this same Lascaris, "who has made himself as obnoxious as a toad," according to Catherine, and who has richly deserved his disgrace. Gross and ignorant as the man is, Falconet prefers to have dealings with him rather than with Betzki.

In the spring of 1770 the model of the statue is finished, and exposed to public view. In order to aid the artist in seizing the movement of a horse standing on his hind legs as if about to spring forward, a groom had for several months, several times a day, made the Empress's two favourite horses, Brilliant and Caprice, prance and curvet under his windows. The head of the hero was modelled by a pupil whom the sculptor had brought with him from Paris, and whom he was to take back with him, to become his daughter-in-law and the consolation of his old age, Mademoiselle Collot. There are several busts signed by the young artist still to be seen at St. Petersburg; but her talent did not fulfil all its promise, for the head of the great Tsar is finely modelled. Probably the master had his share in it too. The success was absolute; every one was deeply impressed. But now began what Falconet called "the years of my impatience," or "the four or five years too much that I remained at St. Petersburg." The transport of the "big stone," which Catherine insisted on getting from a bay near the Gulf of Finland, becomes an affair of state. A reward of seven thousand roubles is offered to any one who will find the means of moving this huge mass weighing five million pounds, and it is the pseudo-Lascaris who earns the reward, by buying the secret, it is said, from a simple-minded blacksmith: an ingenious system of beams hollowed out in grooves, in which run copper balls supporting the huge pyramid. Catherine herself sees the invention put into practice, but the journey of the pyramid lasts a year. From 1770 to 1774, four years more are wasted in trying to find a

caster. Ersman, a Frenchman, who in 1773 undertakes
the job for a sum of a hundred and forty thousand
livres, gets hold of sixty thousand, and decamps without
having done anything to the work. Falconet, losing
all patience, decides on attempting it himself.

As he has never done anything of the kind before,
he spends a year in researches and experiments; at last
he feels confident of success, and, when the moment
comes, his workmen, frightened by the fire that they
themselves have lit, take to flight in the midst of the
casting. The casting is only partially successful; the
head of the rider and the upper part of the horse are
absent. Falconet thinks he can remedy the misfortune
by casting these parts separately. He has no money.
His "impatience" has to last till 1777.

At last the statue is in its place. After having mal-
treated the artist, after criticizing and jeering at his
work, every one is agreed in praising the result of his
heroic labour; and the lines of d'Orbeil meet with
general applause:

> "C'est par tes soins que le bronze respire
> Sur ce rocher de Thétis aperçu,
> Et que le Tsar découvre son empire
> Plus vaste encor qu'il ne l'avait conçu."

But Catherine takes no part in these tardy tributes
of praise. She is away, and thinking of very different
matters. Perhaps she is discontented with the artist for
not having entirely realized the vague dream that she has
had in her head. This horseman in the conventional
tunic, with panther-skin for saddle, this Roman emperor
with the protecting gesture, is not her Peter the Great,

the rude and savage giant that she sees, in so near a
past, hewing out her empire with great strokes of sword
and hatchet, whose path she endeavours to follow. The
rock on which he is placed, the block of granite which
has been brought for her at such expense of time and
money, does not entirely satisfy her. She vaguely
realizes that in shaping and polishing it, in stripping it
of its garb of secular mould, and in striving to give it
an appearance of regularity, the artist has made a mistake. What she had dreamt of was a sublime, heaven-
ward flight of horse and rider, throning the creator
above the work of his hands ; what she sees is a big
stone overpowered by a horse too big for the pedestal,
scarcely lifting the horseman to the level of the first
storey of the neighbouring houses.

Yet, in spite of all, the work is a fine one, and the
visitor who catches sight of it as he arrives at St.
Petersburg, seeing it on high above the river which
Peter brought into the service of his glory, cannot but
feel that it says eloquently, that it personifies powerfully,
some at least of what it was meant to express. And
what human language could express the whole grandeur
and majesty of the living trophies which our history
owes to that other inimitable creator ? Since the day
when Falconet set the statue on its base, generations
have come and gone, and every generation has looked
at horse and rider with an equal enthusiasm. In 1812,
on the news of the threatened invasion, there was some
thought of carrying away the colossus on the desperate
retreat, as the ancient peoples carried their titular deities.

Some one dreamed that he saw the bronze horseman cross the Neva to find the heir of his throne, and bid him fear nothing, since " he protected his city." The statue was left in its place, but Pushkin made use of the vision of Bulhakof in one of the finest poems.

In giving this titular deity to Russia, the inspirer of heroic actions and splendid poems, Falconet sacrificed twelve years of his life, and Russia has never rewarded Falconet, and it is Catherine who is responsible for this injustice. In 1778, weary of waiting for the inauguration of the monument, which seemed to be put off solely for the sake of annoying him, Falconet demands permission to bid farewell to the Empress. She refuses to see him, counts out to him the remainder of the sum agreed upon for his work, and lets him go. He goes back sadly to Paris, where he dies, after having vegetated for a few years in the honours of the Académie de Beaux-Arts. The year after his departure, Catherine uncovers the statue with pompous ceremonials, which she turns into a kind of personal triumph. As for poor Falconet, he counts for nothing in this apotheosis, in which his very name is scarcely recalled.

It is this same Empress, nevertheless, who in 1779 buys from Clérisseau, for a sum of sixty thousand livres, of which he is in need, portfolios of drawings, which she leaves in his keeping, as she had left Diderot his books. Always the same example of the noblest virtues, the virtues most suiting with the rank of Semiramis, practised at a distance. Good architect but bad courtier,

Clérisseau will not accept the imperial gift; he sends the portfolios to St. Petersburg; but he shows his gratitude by demanding of Houdon a bust of the sovereign, whom he names his benefactress, and of whom he wishes to have the likeness in his home.

We have few records in relation to the residence at St. Petersburg of the great sculptor who summed up the last efforts of classic sculpture. The little we know authorizes us to believe that he had no more reason to be content than Falconet. The bust of Catherine, to-day the ornament of one of the most Parisian of salons, that of the Baroness of Romand-Kaissaroff, is enough to explain the reason of the coldness manifested towards the sculptor by the Semiramis of the North. The sculptor of *L'Écorché* was, in his way, a precursor, only too sincere, of the school of modern realists.

That is a school towards which Madame Vigée-Lebrun was certainly not inclined. Her visit to St. Petersburg, however, at the end of Catherine's reign, was not more successful. Was it the forgetfulness, surely pardonable in the agitation of a first interview, of kissing the hand which had been ungloved for that very purpose? Was it some other reason? We cannot say. But the great artist and Semiramis are far from getting on together. A few weeks after the former's arrival, we read in a letter to the "fag":

"Listen, if you please: in the time of Louis XIV., the French school of painting promised to paint nobly, and to unite intellect with charm. Here comes Madame Le Brun in the month of August, as I am returning to

town ; she pretends to be the rival of Angelica Kaufmann, who certainly unites elegance with dignity, and
more ; all her figures have ideal beauty. The rival of
Angelica Kaufmann, for her first attempt, begins by
painting the Grand-Duchesses Alexandrine and Helen.
The former has a dignified and interesting face, with the
air of a queen ; the latter is a perfect beauty, with a
touch of Sainte-Nitouche.   Madame Le Brun squats
you down the two on a sofa, twists the young one's
neck, gives them the air of two *moax* sunning themselves, or, if you will, two ugly little Savoyards with hair
à la Bacchante, with bunches of grapes, and dresses them
in red and violet tunics ; in a word, not only is there
no likeness, but the two sisters are so disfigured that
people ask which is the elder . . .   In this picture there
is neither a likeness, nor taste, nor dignity, and one must
have one's senses stopped up to fail so with such a
subject . . . You should copy Dame Nature, and not
invent the attitudes of apes."

The " senses stopped up," in matters of art, were not
perhaps, in this circumstance, exactly where the great
Empress imagined she found them; and that, to a certain
extent, is her excuse.   Other foreign artists, Benner,
Lampi, Brompton, Koenig, did however enjoy at St.
Petersburg an enviable enough position, from the material
point of view.   But these belonged to a totally different
order ; they had no personal relations with Catherine ;
and the Semiramis of the North has herself defined,
eloquently and peremptorily, the value which she put on
the artists whom she chose to borrow from the neigh-

bouring countries, by charging the "divine" Reiffenstein to send her a couple of Italian architects, "like a bundle of tools."

As for Russian artists of the order of Houdon, Falconet, and Madame Vigée-Lebrun, supposing that she had the occasion of meeting with any, we have spoken at sufficient length elsewhere on the situation in which they found themselves, in describing the death of Lossienko.

CHAPTER III.

I.

MEN of the pen and men of the sword, diplomatists and exalted personages of every kind, the foreign courtiers are legion. To make this chapter complete, we should need to put under contribution a good half of Europe. Some of the foremost nobles of the civilized world, princes and crowned monarchs, appear in the throng, all elbowing one another to come to the front, setting aside their official position in order to attempt a personal conquest, and transacting diplomatic business in the language of Marivaux. Frederick is among them, and, at the time of the first partition of Poland, he vies with even Voltaire:

"The ancient Greeks deified their great men by reserving the chief place to the legislators: they would have placed Your Majesty between Lycurgus and Solon. . . . May my brother express to Your Majesty the admiration in which I hold your great and noble qualities? I have had the felicity of seeing Your Majesty at an age when your charms challenged all those who had

38

any pretensions to beauty. Now, Madame, you are raised above all monarchs and conquerors, among the greatest men that this world has ever seen."

Voltaire too is among the list, and Diderot, and La Harpe. Of these we have already spoken; let us endeavour to glance rapidly at the others.

The agent chosen in 1770 by Frederick, Prince Henry of Prussia, scarcely seemed to possess the required qualities. Madame Sievers, the wife of the statesman whom we have already introduced to the notice of our readers, gives a far from flattering portrait of him : " He is not handsome ; . . . he squints horribly, is short and thin, wears abominably high heels, and a powdered wig to match." She adds, however, that he has intelligence. But this Catherine never seems to discover. If the prince meets with a good reception from her, the charms of his conversation have no more to do with it than the beauty of his wig; it is all on account of the charms of Poland. When he returns, in 1788, the unhappy republic has been already disposed of, and Catherine is more interested in playing with her monkey than in listening to his conversation. It is in vain that Grimm interferes, stating learnedly all the profound political views of the Royal Highness whose friendship he is proud of possessing. The prince is "a busybody, a word-spinner, always on the high horse ; consequential, an arrant gossip; a *petit maître* who leaves the company on the pretence that he has a rendez-vous, and shuts himself up at home." Two years later, Frederick himself is no better treated. Catherine will not even read the hero's recently-published correspondence : " When they brought me this great heap of writings, I chanced upon seventeen pages crammed with downright lies, and when I had read that, I shut the book, and have never looked at the rest." As for the successor, whom Frederick the Great has the misfortune to leave behind him, he is soon put out of count. His first and last appearance at St. Petersburg, in 1780, when he endeavours to make headway against the increasing influence of Austria and the new prestige of Joseph II., is disastrous. The two rivals follow one another at only a few months' interval, and this is what Catherine has to say about them : " I have no advice to give to M. de Falkenstein " (the name under which Joseph travels), " his education is finished, and it would require a very able master to supplement it in any way; but the pretentious novice who has just left here will have to travel far and wide before he comes up to him . . . They say that he has good intentions ; that may be ; but you might say the same of a goose." And when he is on the throne, *Gu*, " fat *Gu*," seems to be her particular aversion. She expends against him almost as boundless a vocabulary of abuse as the complimentary vocabulary of Voltaire. In 1791, hearing that the Emperor, who she knows has become addicted to spiritualism, has had an interview with the spirit of Jesus Christ, she writes to Grimm : " If I could make the acquaintance of the Jew, for it was sure to be a Jew, who played the part of the Saviour, I would make his fortune, on condition that at the second interview he should give him a good drubbing on my behalf."

It was not an easy thing to succeed with the Semiramis

of the North, and it was harder still to keep in her
good graces. The son of Maria Theresa had, however,
a share of this good fortune. Among the strangers
attracted to St. Petersburg by the new " Northern Star,"
Joseph II. seems to have been the only one who aroused
in Catherine that blind and passionate devotion which
gave their passing favour to the most part of her lovers.
He won her fancy, and, for once, the feeling lasted.
Was it absence that brought about this result, by pro-
longing the illusion, in spite of all the tests to which
it was subjected, beyond even death itself ? The
conquest won by Joseph was, at all events, a personal
triumph, and one equally little anticipated on either
side. Both Catherine and he looked forward to their
meeting without the slightest enthusiasm. Catherine,
talking with Grimm, had expressed the opinion that
visitors of this kind were better at home than in travelling all over Europe to put other people to inconvenience; and, in his correspondence with his mother,
while dwelling on the utility of the journey, from which
Maria Theresa augurs no good, which is a little galling
to his pride, and which causes him to dread the " tricks
of the Greek faith," Joseph is cold, sceptical, and sarcastic. It is a political manœuvre that he is anxious to
play off, and he has already converted old Kaunitz to
his way of thinking, so far indeed as to set him making
plans on paper for the partition of Turkey. But he
intends to present himself as courtier and not as
sovereign; " he will content himself with a place in the
great Empress's ante-room," where he can " increase the
number of those who are admitted to admire her glory

and her virtues": so he writes to Kaunitz in a letter meant to be shown. And he strictly carries out his programme : at Mohilef, and afterwards at Tsarskoïe, he affects the strictest incognito. He puts up in an inn which is improvised for him by putting up a sign-board on a bathing-tent near the imperial palace, and there installing Catherine's English gardener as innkeeper. He sleeps on a sack which he has brought among his baggage, and which he stuffs with straw.

The inn and the sack are lucky discoveries on his part, for Catherine is one of those who are easily impressed by traits of this kind. But Joseph has other means, one especially, which he explains openly, cynically almost, to his chancellor : " Her vanity must be tickled ; her vanity is her idol ; boundless luck and the extravagant flattery of all Europe have turned her head ; one must go with the crowd." He does not fail to do so. Taken by Patiomkin to the house in which she is living at Mohilef, he waits patiently till she has come back from mass ; then he rushes forward, and would kiss her hand. And he is careful to say nothing at first in regard to his real intentions ; he considers her "by no means inclined to reason out things in politics." He endeavours to interest, amuse, and, above all, flatter her. He only quits the tone of light *badinage* in order to take that of respectful gallantry, with just a touch of sentiment. He succeeds admirably. When he leaves, she is entirely won over, and for good. She writes to her confidant: " I should never end, if I began to sing his praises ; he has the most solid, profound, and well-informed intelligence that I have ever come across ; you would have to get up early in order to get ahead of him." And a little later she writes: "I know a man to whom heaven has destined the foremost place in Europe, without doubt the foremost. He must live, and survive two of his contemporaries"—herself and Frederick, without doubt, for she is not the one to forget herself, even in her rhapsodies—"and then his star will have no rival, he will leave all his contemporaries far behind."

Nor has she been able to resist the temptation of discussing with such a man more serious subjects than those with which he has entertained her. That is where he had hoped to lead her, and she comes to it the first. Without abandoning the air of affected lightness which they have adopted by mutual consent, pretending even to have turned aside on a false scent, she asks him what is going on in Italy. Has not the ambition of a sovereign like himself ever turned in that direction? Does not Rome seem to him the natural capital of the Emperor of the Romans? And Constantinople the natural capital of an Empress of the East? replies Joseph, finding the moment apt for his purpose. Then the conversation changes again; they spend five hours "in chattering and roaring with laughter, whilst Europe is all ears to know what they have to say to one another" in so lengthy a *tête-à-tête*. But the ice is broken; during the next few days Joseph sees with satisfaction that the Empress "turns around the subject more and more," and, when he takes his leave, the future alliance and the future campaign against Turkey are already half planned.

There were many conjectures in the air, as they were seen so anxious to please and then so visibly pleased by one another, and Catherine complacently reports to Grimm: "People have been saying, as we are always together, hanging on one another's words, that we are going to get married." And there was indeed to be a certain union, arising from this few weeks' intimacy, a union of policy and ambition, in which, on the side of Catherine at least, there was more of the heart than the head ; in which diplomatic formalities were entirely forgotten, or set contemptuously aside, in which the minister of foreign affairs had no part or lot, in which no protocol was exchanged, so that Frederick's representative, reassured by Panin, was completely taken in, and assured his master that Catherine had seen nothing in her imperial guest but an "indiscreet gossip," and that Count Falkenstein had done very little for the interests of Joseph II. !

A correspondence followed, in which Catherine declared that " pagan antiquity, deifying heroes, was justified in her eyes from the charge of flattery " ; and the rôle remained the same on the one side and the other ; a sincere exaltation on the side of the Empress, and a cold calculation on that of the Emperor ; Catherine's letters being corrected by André Shuvalof, a poet ; Joseph's by Kaunitz.

Nevertheless this union contracted under such happy auspices was not quite a success. And, by a caprice of fortune, which, somehow, was always on her side, or by a supreme irony of fate, this association of interests to which Catherine contributed, in the opinion of Joseph, too much fantasy and femininity, while he himself put only calculation, was disastrous mainly to him ; all the profit was on her side. He does not succeed in utilizing the good-will of his imperial friend either in his project of bartering the Netherlands against Bavaria, or in his difference with Holland. In 1786 he has a moment of discouragement and ill-humour. A letter of Catherine asking for his support at Constantinople, when she has just agreed to the mediation of France, and begging him, in a postscript, "to follow her to Kherson," strikes him as being decidedly too "cavalier." He proposes to send back a reply which shall be "brief and straightforward, but which shall show this Catherinized Princess of Zerbst that she ought to be less summary in her way of disposing of an Emperor." He sends his reply. Catherine replies calmly enough, saying that she is quite sure he will come to the Crimea ; and he comes. It is he who perseveres in unshaken fidelity to a compact which, in his case, is not worth keeping ; it is he who clings closest to it, through all the ordeals of the unfortunate campaign, in which the Turks seem resolved to avenge on him and his forces every defeat which they meet with at the hands of Catherine. He complains, in 1789, in his correspondence with Kaunitz, of "the absurdity and impertinence" of his ally's behaviour ; but in the following year, on his death-bed, he dictates a letter to her in which we meet with such phrases as these: "I shall never again see the writing of Your Imperial Majesty, which has been all my happiness to me, and I feel all the bitterness of knowing that this is the last time I can assure you of my tender regard."

No doubt he is not sincere even now, and Kaunitz is right in seeing a masterpiece of heroism in the last effort of an actor leaving the scene on which he is never to reappear, but playing his part to the very end. What matter, if the illusion is complete, and the effect carried out? It is one of Catherine's finest victories. For her, this death is a really sincere distress, but it is especially an immense surprise. She cannot get over it for a long time. "Born and bred for his place in the world, full of wit, talent, and knowledge, how has he managed to reign so badly, not only without success, but in such a way as to be reduced to the unfortunate state in which he died?" Grimm, whom she thus interrogates, does not inform her of a scene in a burlesque, much like the *revues de fin d'année* of the present day, which was played at a Berlin theatre in 1785, in which a courier enters with two big bags of dispatches, one in front and one behind.

"What have you got there?"

"The orders of the Emperor."

"And there?"

"The orders countermanded."

The agreement signed so gaily at Mohilef in 1780 was never countermanded by the unfortunate Emperor, and Catherine was alone in not seeing in his character a trait which sufficiently explains the whole lamentable history of her hero.

She showed more insight in regard to Gustavus of Sweden. Near relatives (the father of one and the mother of the other were brother and sister), they had certain characteristics in mind and temperament which have a distinct family likeness. Both of them ambitious, with an equal sense of their own place and rank in the world, an equal taste for imposing on the imagination of the crowd, they were both singularly influenced by Western culture, and, in particular, by French literature. But, as some one has observed, the same tendencies and appetites take a feminine turn with the King, a masculine turn with his cousin. The first care of Gustavus is to shine ; the means are of little consequence. He can be satisfied, if need be, with diamonds, with which he likes to cover himself on state occasions ; Catherine is not so easily satisfied.

The first visit of the " Count of Gothland " to St. Petersburg in 1777 puts them, however, on somewhat intimate terms. Gustavus claims the right to call his cousin by the Russian name of *siestra* (sister) ; on his return to Stockholm, he sends her presents of books, and receives in return the title of member of the Imperial Academy. He has taken a liking to the national delicacies of *kvass* and *shtchi ;* a man skilled in .preparing them is sent to him. But Catherine's mind is made up about her guest, and the opinion is no favourable one. This "gentleman spending the day before the mirror" has nothing to say to her of any value. And, while she is lavish with her cajoleries to the *brat* (brother), who returns them with an equally lavish hand, she endeavours secretly to undermine the order of things which, in 1772, has saved Sweden and its king by a *coup d'État* which gives the one the absolute mastery over the other.

In 1783 they meet again at Friedrichshamn, and

Catherine receives a still worse impression than before.
On his way to the place of meeting, Gustavus falls
from his horse as he is reviewing the troops, and breaks
his arm.   What clumsiness! "Fancy doing a somer-
sault before one's troops!"   They part apparently on
the most friendly terms, and it is still amiably enough
that Catherine, next year, asks the King if it is true,
as the report goes, that he is going to march his forces
into Finland in order to "take them to supper at St.
Petersburg"?   But the approaching rupture is already
in the air.   Gustavus, in spite of the good advice urged
upon him by the Cabinet of Versailles, writes that "one
must have a war to characterize a reign."   He seizes
the favourable occasion that the second Turkish war
seems to offer.   We know the rest.   From 1788 to
1790 hostilities are carried on by sea—and on paper.
Catherine expends floods of ink.   The peace of August
14, 1790, does not arrange things quite satisfactorily.
Catherine is only half reconciled to an adversary who
has come out more than half conqueror from the strife,
and is far from charmed by the costume in which Gustavus makes his appearance in a "temple of friendship,"
"hastily set up," says Langeron, "with three or four
boards, decorated with his cipher and that of the Empress, and guarded by some soldiers dressed as Bacchus,
their faces stained with wine-lees."   The costume is,
indeed, a little startling, even to eyes accustomed to
the costumes of Prince Patiomkin: "a short Swedish
coat, embroidered all round the edges, with three lace
ruffles and three rows of epaulettes, the last of which
comes to the elbow; very tight silk breeches, half blue

and half yellow, laced boots, the immense spurs of
Charles XII., and his sword suspended from an enormous shoulder-belt, two scarves, all his orders on his
coat, and, to put the finishing touch, a yellow straw
hat with a huge blue feather in it."

Matters were not finally patched up between the
Empress and this "harlequin king" until the time of
the anti-revolutionary campaign of 1792, when Catherine was ready to snatch at anything in order to cut a
decent figure without interfering with her own affairs
in Poland. And thereupon she returned to the former
fraternal caresses, flattering and cajoling the half-heroic,
half-burlesque heir of Charles XII., playing upon his
feverish pride, and setting him dreaming of "sailing up
the Seine on gun-boats." The pistol-shot of Ankas-
troem (March 16, 1792) puts an end to these imaginary
journeys.

II.

Though neither king nor emperor, the Prince de
Ligne deserves a place of honour in this company. To
properly indicate his place there, would require a separate book. Catherine must have singularly enjoyed
the society of this cosmopolitan, who had precisely the
kind of charm and intelligence to which she was most
alive. "The Prince de Ligne is here," she writes to
Grimm in September 1780, "one of the most pleasant
men, and the easiest to get on with, that I have ever
met. He is really quite a character; he thinks pro-

foundly, and behaves like a child." She does not treat
him quite fairly in 1787, in sending him to Patiomkin's
head-quarters "to play the spy," as she says cynically,
when he has been expecting "orders to take Belgrade."
But he is the first to find himself out of place in this
position, and he has little difficulty in making his own
defence. His correspondence with Catherine has not
yet, unfortunately, been published in its entirety. Some
of his letters, which have only appeared in a Russian
publication, are extremely curious, and highly instructive in studying his personality. Those written in
October 1792, immediately after the death of a be-
loved son, throw into vivid relief the characteristics
of this courtier *par excellence :* the father, deeply and
sincerely distressed as he is, is never for a moment
apparent, there is not a single heartfelt word in it,
nothing but the courtier, who makes phrases, always
after the same pattern: " I write, not to Your Imperial
Majesty, but to a heavenly being . . . Why did he
not die under the walls of Ismaïl? Why did not I
myself fall under the walls of Otchakof?" And again:
" How can I express my gratitude to Your Imperial
Majesty for the flowers which she has deigned to lay
on the tomb of my poor Charles? . . . One who is
more deserving of praise than Trajan can well pro-
nounce a funeral oration . . . Your Majesty is a very
Bossuet, a very Robertson." Nothing is wanting, not
even compliments to Plato Zubof.

The Prince de Ligne pretended to have followed
Catherine, in 1787, through the Crimea as a sort of
" diplomatic jockey." The Comte de Ségur, who was

the official representative of diplomacy, expended a larger amount of madrigals and *bouts-rimés* than of official qualities. There was no chance of success in the diplomatic line, save in such procedures. It was Catherine's taste, and also her method—for it is one of the signs of ability to turn one's natural inclinations, and even one's weaknesses, into means of action—to treat grave subjects lightly, and to give a pleasant turn to the most thorny questions. The serious side of things had its turn when the moment came for action ; then there were no more pleasantries. When the partition of Poland was to be carried out, Catherine joked with Prince Henry, exchanged compliments with Frederick, and then, when the moment was come, Kretchetnikof received his orders, very precise and very little pleasing, and the hapless republic was seized by the throat and strangled by the hands of a dragoon.

"I am not surprised at M. de Ségur's reputation," wrote the Empress in 1785, on the arrival of the brilliant young diplomatist whom the Cabinet of Versailles had discovered ; "it seems to me richly deserved, and certainly the best result of anything you have yet sent me from your country. It is difficult to be more amiable or more witty. He seems happy amongst us, and is as gay as a lark. He has written songs and verses for us." There is still a specimen of the poetic skill of the gay diplomatist on a marble column in the park of Tsarskoïe, erected in memory of the charming *Zémire*, a greyhound, whose loss was so great a grief to Catherine, and who should not have been taken from his mistress's side, for the gods

> " Devaient à sa fidelité
> Le don de l'immortalité
> Pour qu'elle fût toujours auprès de sa maîtresse."

Ségur was not always so happy as this, and his muse
sometimes comes to grief, as in this flattering portrait of
Catherine :

> " Je veux en peu de mots peindre un grand empereur ;
> L'entreprise est facile en paraissant hardie :
> Son cachet fournira les pinceaux, la couleur ;
> Sa devise peindra son cœur."

He was most successful in his *bouts-rimés*.   Those
composed on the four rhymes, *amour, tambour, frotte,* and
note, given by the English envoy, Fitz-Herbert, are
justly famous :

> " D'un peuple très-heureux Catherine est *l'amour ;*
> Malheur à l'ennemi qui contre elle se *frotte ;*
> La renommée aura pour elle son *tambour ;*
> L'histoire avec plaisir sera son *garde-note.*"

All this was improvised between two promenades
under the trees of Tsarskoïe, or between two relays on
the road from St. Petersburg to Moscow. For just then,
from 1785 to 1787, Catherine was in the humour for
travelling, and it was in accompanying her across the
deserts of the vast empire that Ségur first made his
reputation as a man of wit, a man of the world, and a
wary diplomatist. He did credit to his task, and was
not slow in reaping the reward of his endeavours.
Admitted at once to the inner circle of the Hermitage,
he was soon the ornament of a society to which his
colleague from Vienna, Cobenzl, contributed only the
amusement of his folly, where Léon Naryshkin, in

company with Matrena Danilovna, the court fool, poured out his stock of vulgar buffooneries, and where one saw courtiers of the type that Griboïedof put on the stage, gouty and feeble old men, risking the safety of their arms and legs for the sovereign's amusement, and not always with impunity, in their endeavour to keep pace with the gambols of Naryshkin.

The Crimean journey fully established the favour of the new-comer. Perhaps, this time, the courtier prevailed a little too strongly over the politician. Ségur looked on Catherine, and on the new country through which he travelled by her side, with the eyes of a lover. He was convinced, as we see from his memoirs, that there were no poor in Russia, and that the condition of the serfs was quite enviable. It was only on hearing the mournful songs of the *burlaks*, rowing the barges on the Dnieper, that he discovered some signs of the long slavery undergone by this " free tribe of primitive Scythians." He read some of Catherine's writings during the journey, and showed a suitable interest in them ; but he does not seem to have so much as realized the existence of any other Russian literature. The glitter of the " Northern Star " eclipsed in his eyes everything outside the radius of that luminous sphere. At Kief his muse awoke once more, and an inscription for the portrait painted by Shebanof, a serf of Patiomkin, once more won for him the smiles of Semiramis :

> " Si le sort n'avait su lui donner un empire,
>   Elle aurait eu toujours un trône dans nos cœurs."

It was not till 1789 that this perfect harmony between the Empress and the diplomatist was broken. Whose

fault was it ?   It is a doubtful question.   The first note
of discord crept in on the subject of revolutionary ideas ;
but two years earlier they were quite in union on this
point : Ségur having said that La Fayette was a friend
of his, Catherine invited La Fayette to join him at Kief !
In 1789 Ségur is still faithful to his former sentiments ;
he writes such enthusiastic letters to the commandant
of the *garde-nationale* that Catherine, reading them in
her " black cabinet," is amazed : " Can a minister of the
king write in that strain ? "   Perhaps she sees ahead,
and the time is soon to come when Ségur will think
with her.   There is at this time no kind of ill-will in the
sovereign's reserve ; and in her reflections on the subject there is more of sorrow than of anger.   " I have no
doubt whatever as to the sincerity of the Comte de
Ségur's feelings in regard to me," she writes to Grimm ;
" he is a man of honour, uprightness, and nobility."
Two years later, when Génet takes up the heavy responsibility of the succession to his place, as *chargé d'affaires*,
he denies the truth of the " absurd rumours " which have
been circulated in reference to the disgrace incurred by
his predecessor, rumours which at St. Petersburg have
only called forth the " pity " of the better-informed
people, and " the indignation of Catherine."   But, this
time, he is, or chooses to be, mistaken, for his dispatch,
dated the 31st of May, 1791, has been forestalled
by a letter from Catherine to Grimm, dated the
2nd of May, in which we read : " There is one man
whose whimsies I cannot forgive, and that is Ségur.
Shame on him ! he is false as Judas, and I am not at all
surprised that no one likes him in France.   One must

have an opinion of one's own in this world, and the man who has none is only to be despised. What part will he play in regard to the Pope? The same that he had played here with me, leaving here after daubing one with all the axioms of the ancient chivalry of France, after pretending that he was in despair at the turn things were taking : what does he do, once in Paris?"

We may doubt whether Ségur was really so well posted up in what was going on in Paris, after all. He had only left his post on account of his impatience to fling himself into the *mêlée*. But, on the other hand, not knowing what was to happen, alike in regard to the Revolution and to the part he proposed to play in it, he had only asked for leave of absence for a few months; he had declared himself ready to return to St. Petersburg at the first intimation from her, "like a courier," and, for this reason alone, the farewell words that he puts in the mouth of Catherine, in which she condemns the revolutionary movement and regrets to see him associated with it, do not seem very plausible. Probably on both sides they refrained from coming to such a definite explanation. Subsequent events speak for themselves. The movement which Ségur was dying to fling himself into carried him with it much further than he intended, or than Catherine could have foreseen, and forced him into certain compromises and double dealings which he would have shrunk from only a few months before. "With some," writes the Empress to Grimm, "he passes for a democrat, with others for an autocrat, and finally he is one of the first to rush off to the Hôtel de Ville to subscribe to that fine oath ; after which he goes to

Rome, apparently to present himself to the Pope as a self-excommunicated man . . . It was the *Comte de Ségur* whom we saw here, and who brought back the court of Louis XIV. again . . . Now it is *Louis Ségur* who is infected with the national disease."

It is the characteristic of great crises, from which some new political or social ideal is to spring, that they disconcert the most far-seeing of intellects, and warp the most upright of characters.

III.

The numerous readers whom M. Maugras has recently charmed and interested would not forgive me if I were not to mention here the name of Lauzun, although all that we know of his relations with Catherine is the little that he himself tells us in his memoirs, and that little surpasses greatly the limits of the most indulgent credulity. He went to Poland in 1774, with the twofold aim of winning the favour of the Princess Czartoryska and of being appointed French minister at Warsaw. He may well have succeeded in the first of these two endeavours, which does not seem to have been difficult of attainment; when he was certain of not being able to succeed in the second, he set himself, after the then fashion, to play the diplomatist on his own account. As the King declined the benefit of being officially represented by him, he assumed, on his own account, the position of unofficial representative of the Queen. He dreamt of bringing about something like a personal

alliance between this princess and the mighty autocrat
of the North. Catherine is supposed to have at first
looked favourably on his advances, even to the point
of giving him " unlimited powers " ; then, changing her
mind, to have asked him to enter her own service. In
what capacity ? By offering him " the highest position
to which a subject could rise " in her empire, we read in
the memoirs of the hero. Was it then the position of
Patiomkin or of Plato Zubof ? And it is on hearing
of this brilliant prospect that Marie Antoinette would
appear to have made the sad reflection : " The Empress
of Russia is indeed happy, and I most unhappy."

Perhaps M. Maugras' second volume will enlighten us
on this subject. Lauzun wrote to Catherine : so much
is certain. And she replied to him : that at least is
probable. It was not in the usual way of Semiramis
to put off any one. Few there were whom she failed to
respond to. When, in 1780, the good Abbé de Lubersac sent her the plan of a monument to erect at St.
Petersburg, with the inscription, " *Catharine II. Thetis
altera*," she did not tell him what she thought of it ; she
put the drawing—a huge water-colour, three feet and a
half by two feet and a half—in her gallery, sent a medal
to the artist, and thought no more about it. Lord
Findlater, an English original, of the kind that was then
plentiful in all parts of Europe, living in Saxony, where
his eccentricities and his bounties were alike the delight
of the country, going every year to take the waters at
Carlsbad, where the people were almost ready to raise
a statue in his honour, and professing a boundless admiration for the Semiramis of the North, was equally well

received. She did not always read the plans for the reconstruction of Europe which he sent to her through the inevitable " fag," but she was not above making use of him in matters of less importance, the settlement of her grand-daughters in Germany, for instance.

Her medals, which she distributed so liberally as to somewhat lessen their value, were none the less extremely prized. There is, however, one instance to the contrary. In 1786 the Comte de Ségur received from a Comte de Turpin, author of a work on Cæsar's Commentaries, a letter couched in these terms : " When I took the liberty of sending my work to Her Imperial Majesty, I had no other design than to do homage to her virtues, talents, and learning, and I never thought that this homage was likely to receive or to deserve a present from Her Imperial Majesty. . . . The medal that you are good enough to inform me of, well worthy of respect as it is, coming from the hand of Her Imperial Majesty, could not be accepted by the Comte de Turpin, were it worth a hundred thousand écus. My principles, and those of all French gentlemen, would not permit me to receive any present from a foreign power." Gentlemen of this kind were not numerous in France, whatever the author of this letter may have thought, and Catherine was never fortunate enough to meet with another.

CHAPTER IV.

THE FRENCH AT THE NORTHERN COURT.

I.

THE Comte de Turpin had few imitators. Not all of those drawn towards Russia by the fame and fortune of Semiramis aspired to the *rôle* that Voltaire would like to have played, in succession to Diderot, and which was so well played by Joseph II.; some being too modest in rank, others too little inclined to play the part of courtier. For there was a flocking thither of all kinds and from all quarters, and I should be attempting too great a task if I endeavoured to deal in detail with all this influx. Forced to choose, I shall choose the French, who were at once the most numerous and the most interesting of the contingent.

The reign of Elizabeth had already induced some to brave the inclemency of so trying a climate, and the still more hazardous surprises of an uncertain career in an unknown country; under Catherine the tide definitely sets in. At the same time, a few Russians make their way to Paris, only very few as yet; outside the diplomatic world there are only two or three who pay

more than a mere tourist's visit, a certain Karjavin for
instance, who is a curious, almost a unique type, the
first of a series. He is not, indeed, the future boyard
of legend, an anything but attractive creature; he is
something much better than that. Son of a St. Petersburg merchant, he finishes his studies in London and
in Paris, where, in 1755, he attends the Sorbonne, in
1760, the Collège des Étrangers. On his return to
Russia he is appointed professor of French at the
University of Moscow, where he takes the place of a
Frenchman named Lavis, who has been living in the
country for the last forty-five years. This too is a new
beginning: Russia is soon to spare the expense of
getting its professors from foreign countries. In 1773
Karjavin is once more on the banks of the Seine: he
has had a quarrel with his father, who has tried to make
a merchant of him. And now, even at Paris, necessity
forces him to engage in this detested occupation. He
has married a Parisian, and he has difficulty in making
both ends meet. In 1776 he embarks for Martinique
with a French passport and some merchandise. But
business is no more successful than it is agreeable to
him: his stock is pillaged on the way by an English
cruiser. He tries his hand at everything; turns chemist
at Martinique, where Duprat, the King's apothecary,
offers him the reversion of his place. His establishment
is destroyed by a flood. He becomes in turn interpreter
to the Admiralty, tobacconist, clerk on a French
victualler, doctor on a Spanish ship. In 1788 he
returns to France, under the name of Lamy, then he
once more goes back to Russia. Meanwhile he publishes

a number of books, French translations of Russian works (*Voyage du Spitzberg, Instructions Chrétiennes, Mythologie russo-slavonne*) ; an essay, in Russian, on architecture, for he is also an architect ; a description, in French, of "a louse under the microscope" (Paris, 1789), for he is also an entomologist.

Let us not laugh : the specialization of talents is a late growth in every nation, and of the many Frenchmen who sought their fortune in Russia, at the time when this Russian endeavoured to earn his living in France, few indeed did so much honourable work. Bernardin de Saint-Pierre himself, whose name naturally occurs in this connection, loses by the comparison.

Every one knows the story of this anything but idyllic enterprise, to which the enthusiastic Aimé Martin has vainly endeavoured to lend some charm. His journey from Paris to St. Petersburg is that of a mere *chevalier d'industrie*, travelling from stage to stage at the expense of the first person he comes across on the road. On his arrival at the capital of the North, the future creator of an immortal work has in his pocket an écu of six livres, and an engineer's certificate which has been given to him by mistake. It is true that he has a wonderful dream in his head, a sort of semi-mythological royalty in an empire which, with the aid of Catherine, he proposes to create on the banks of the Caspian. The grand-master of artillery, Villebois, whose favour he succeeds in gaining, endeavours to change this chimera into a reality by setting the youth and interest of the new-comer to checkmate Gregory Orlof. It is a vain attempt. There is a little journey through Finland, where another Frenchman, General du Bosquet, in charge of the military defences of the littoral, puts the knowledge of the adventurous engineer to the test, with the most unfavourable results; a fresh series of loans, which finally tire out the generosity of a third compatriot, the court jeweller Duval; a final discouragement, a hasty retreat in the direction of Warsaw; and we are at the end of this scarcely glorious Odyssey. It takes place, it is true, in 1765, and Bernardin has still twenty years of fruitless vagabondage to go through before the day of *Paul et Virginie*.

Villebois, du Bosquet, and Duval are survivals, at the court of Catherine, of the epoch which has gone before. They attain little prominence, and leave no trace behind them. Their successors are for the most part equally unimportant. There is Clerc, or Le Clerc, a Franche-Comtois, who, after being physician in the house of the Duc de Orléans at Villers Cotterets, passes in 1759 into the service of the *hetman* Razumovski, becomes in 1769 physician to the Grand-Duke Paul, then, successively, scholastic director of the Imperial Corps des Cadets, inspector of the hospital of St. Paul at Moscow, and, unable after all to acclimatize himself in his country of adoption, goes back to France after making his fortune, and is ennobled by Louis XVI.

There is the Lyonnese Patrin, a mineralogist of some importance, who, from 1780 to 1787, makes valuable researches in Siberia, without, like the Abbé de Chappe, drawing on himself the displeasure of Catherine, but not without arousing the jealous animosity of the German geographer, Pallas. Ségur mentions in his memoirs another traveller, bearing a name which has since become illustrious, Jean de Lesseps, the grandfather of the constructor of the Suez Canal, appointed consul at Kronstadt at the age of seventeen, one of La Pérouse's companions in 1782, but, luckily for himself, sent on shore at Kamschatka with dispatches which he brings back to St. Petersburg in 1788, "zealous, ardent, indefatigable," and only anxious to set out once more.

There is, too, a Sieur Viridet, calling himself a citizen of Geneva, but apparently born at Paris, who is concerned in 1786 with the editorship of the first French newspaper printed in Russia, the *Mercure de Russie*, in which one finds a little of everything, except sense and judgment; verses like these, for instance, composed in 1787 in celebration of the return of Catherine to St. Petersburg after her journey through the Crimea :

> " Pis comm' je n' savons pas feindre,
> J' conviendrions bonnement
> Qu'all' a su se faire craindre
> A ces porteux de turbans ;
> I l'y parlerions de guerre
> Et d' ces braves généraux,
> Qui d'sus l'eau comme sur terre
> Ont fait tant d'exploits nouveaux."

This is entitled : *Chanson poissarde sur le retour de sa Majesté.*

One of Viridet's collaborateurs on the *Mercure* is a Chevalier de la Traverse. The tone of the journal, naturally, is resolutely conservative, more and more so indeed as the revolutionary crisis develops. Certain *Stances sur la liberté* appear in it, intended no doubt

to warn the Frenchmen in Russia against these dangerous disorders :

> " La liberté qui vous tourne la tête
> Est selon vous un très grand bien.
> Ah ! pardonnez, je n'en crois rien ;
> J'aime le calme, et j'ai vu la tempête."

Catherine, too, " loves the calm " at this moment, and
she is not critical of the way in which her glories are
sung.   In regard to French men of letters, she takes
what comes, welcoming the waifs and strays of the
great literary tempest from which the Revolution arose.
She receives even Abraham Chaumeix himself, shunned
as he is by the encyclopædists, and ill-treated by
Voltaire in person.   She allows him to establish a
school at Moscow, where he dies in 1790.   She even
makes, at his request, a new regulation, which must
be put down to the lasting credit of the poor refugee,
for it puts an end to one of the disgraces of Russia by
prescribing decent measures for the burial of the poor,
whom Chaumeix has been horrified at seeing thrown
into the common sewer.   The subjects of the sovereign,
the great lords of both capitals, are not too particular.
Casanova meets at the table of Count Tshernishof a
French lackey whom he has brought with him to St.
Petersburg, and whom he has discharged on account
of misconduct : the lackey has become a tutor.   A
French cook demands the vacant place of director of
the Académie des Beaux-Arts ; he declares that he
has had a scullion under his orders who is now a teacher
of languages in the house of Count Sheremetief.   French
cooks, pastry-cooks, and barbers abound in this land

where big fortunes are so readily to be made. In 1789 the favourite Lanskoï has the famous confectioner Babu sent to him from Paris by Grimm. Nor should the actors and actresses be forgotten. Mademoiselle Huss carried off by Count Markof from the Comédie Française, where Grimm complained that she followed too closely in Mademoiselle Clairon's steps, and conspired with her to "lose for the second time the taste for the true declamation, established by Baron and Mademoiselle Lecouvreur," has nothing but triumphs of all kinds on the banks of the Neva. Near the capital, at Pavlovsk, a certain street, *Pikof piereoulok*, recalls vaguely to-day the name of an artist, doubly famed, as composer and as executant, for a marvellous ballet and an extraordinary solo, danced on the 28th of April, 1791, at the famous ball given at the palace of Taurida by the most splendid of princes to the most glorious of empresses.

These hardy seekers of fortune do not always meet with success. Lafosse, the famous veterinary surgeon, who, after attending to His Most Christian Majesty's stables before becoming a revolutionary, finds himself at St. Petersburg in 1789, just at the right moment for attending to a marvellous horse belonging to Prince Patiomkin, a present from the Emperor Joseph, succeeds in curing the horse, but not in getting paid for it, and, on insisting too emphatically, is only too happy to get out of the affair by clearing the frontier.

Glad and happy to welcome people with any kind of artistic recommendation, giving hospitality, in 1782, to M. de Buffon, whom she receives " as the son of an illustrious man, that is to say *sans façons*," as she says to Grimm, and delighted to show him the bust of his father in the gallery at Tsarskoïe, Catherine is less amiable towards certain gentlemen of more or less importance who make more or less to-do in her capital, and bring discredit on the name of France. In 1765 she writes to Madame Geoffrin :

" They say here that M. de Conflans had some intelligence, and decided talent as a soldier, that he drank too much punch, that he told a great many lies, that he deceived his father (who is said to be an excellent man), that he was too self-confident, but that, if he could get over these little defects, he would really deserve to be called one of the hopes of France, as a soldier, you understand. If one sends him as ambassador to Poland, he will come to grief, and will not fail to return me my compliments, for all your people in office say the most awful things about me."

In 1765, let us remember, we are but at the beginning of the great reign, and the propaganda of Voltaire and his friends has not yet done its work. The popularity which the Semiramis of the North is soon to enjoy at Paris, will have its periods of variation, and Catherine is always very sensitive on this subject. In 1783 and 1789 she is very much annoyed by reports circulated in regard to her health. She is said to be suffering from cancer, and she is as much offended as if it were the gravest insult. She does not forgive Frederick for believing, or affecting to believe, the report. On making inquiries, she finds out that it arises from a certain court lady who has had several consultations by correspondence with the celebrated surgeon, Louis. She sends a detailed description of her malady, and the document somehow gets about. There is a certain English turn about some of the phrases, and people immediately set it down to the Empress's physician, Rogerson ; in the description of the lady it is stated that "she is a widow, and has lived a fast life," and the scandal-mongers need no more proof that it is the widow of Peter III. This is enough to arouse a much less friendly welcome than usual to the Frenchmen who venture just now to make their way into Russia, and the letters sent to the Empress's Parisian correspondent show traces enough of the feeling. "Do tell me," she writes in December 1783, "why you need send me such uninteresting people. There are half-a-dozen here whom you might as well have kept at home : it would have been no loss to the world in general . . . What was the good of springing upon us a Comte de Caraman, for instance, an economist and a duffer, who has only worried the life out of the Grand Chamberlain, and added to all the ills and ailments of everybody else without rhyme or reason ? You had better burst him and put him in a bladder, when he shall sail over our heads in broad daylight."

The discovery of balloons was at this time causing great excitement at the capital of the North, greatly to Catherine's disapproval ; after a short time she forbade the continuation of experiments which seemed to her equally dangerous and useless ; but the fancy for flying through the air is not the complaint she has most often to make against the compatriots of the Comte de Caraman. In 1784 a Comte de Verneuil, formerly lieutenant in a regiment of cavalry, and ex-chevalier of St. Lazare, for he has been deprived of his decoration, is received in the most brilliant society at St. Petersburg. He has good manners, sings well, and accompanies himself on the clavecin, and appears to be rich. Presently the plate disappears from one house, valuable watches and snuff-boxes from jewellers' windows ; and after some months the culprit is discovered. He is referred to Versailles, and Louis XVI. replies that he leaves him in the hands of justice in the country where he has dishonoured his own ; but meanwhile he has succeeded in escaping. He reaches the frontier without a passport, and plays his cards so adroitly that the governor of the locality puts him into a *kibitka*, and sends him on to the first German station ; three hours later a courier arrives with the warrant for his arrest. In the following year, another chevalier of St. Lazare, giving himself out to be the Comte de Bussy, arrives from Poland, where he is supposed to have married a Princess Radziwill. He turns out to be an adventurer who has escaped from prison in Copenhagen, after a career of swindling in Poland and Sweden. Then there is a Marquis d'Archies, a relative of the Ducs de Guines and de Ghistel ; a young knight bearing the name of the Vicomte de Cromard and the gendarme's uniform, "without being able to prove that he has any right to one or the other ; " a Sieur Daubray, formerly lawyer to the Parliament of Metz, who is banished from the country for reasons which the Comte de Ségur, on his arrival at St. Petersburg, thinks it as well not to inquire into too closely, for, as he writes to the Comte de Vergennes : "My principles and yours, monsieur, forbid me to take the slightest interest in those Frenchmen who respect so little either the laws of honour or the reputation of their country."

II.

It was due to the Comte de Ségur that a desirable change came about in the character of the French pretenders to imperial favour. From this time forward, the dubious bearers of the cross of St. Lazare are few and far between in the Northern capital, and Catherine at the same time makes the acquaintance of the most genuine and worthy members of the French aristocracy, of which she was in danger of receiving a very inaccurate and a very unpleasant idea. In 1777 she had had one single good fortune of the kind ; and she wrote to Grimm :

"I forgot to tell you that the Vicomte de Laval Montmorency has been here, and, though he is not perhaps the finest gentleman in the world, still he is the first Frenchman I have met whose manners were not insupportable. . . . And I have also paid him as much honour as I could, because he is a Montmorency, and it is a name one likes to hear. I wish they would make him marshal of France ; I believe he knows as much about war as most."

The Comte de Ségur has the pleasure of multiplying these agreeable impressions. Introduced by him at the

court of Semiramis, the Marquis de Jumilhac, the Comte
d'Aguesseau, and yet others, win general esteem, that
of Catherine included.   Then follow the volunteers
attracted to the Russian armies by the second Turkish
war and the Swedish war; and, despite the suspicions
which the Empress has at this moment in regard to the
dubious attitude of the Cabinet of Versailles, they meet
with the most favourable reception on her part. She
keeps them at a certain distance, refuses any sort of
intimacy with them, but is quite ready to encourage
their efforts in her service.   The Comte de Lameth,
who is presented to her in the course of the Crimean
journey, leaves her, when he returns to Suvorof's
camp, under the charm of a grace and wit which,
apart from Ségur himself, she rarely meets with in
her usual society.   She little thinks at that time that
three years later the *Gazette de Saint-Pétersbourg* will
print these lines: "The Comte de Lameth and other
rebels, enemies not only of the King, but of the nation,
have amused themselves at the head of a drunken
rabble beneath the windows of the King and Queen at
the Tuileries."

Ségur has brought before us picturesquely enough the
first appearance of the brilliant officer before the chief
under whom Catherine desires that he should enter her
service:

"What nationality are you?"

"French."

"What profession?"

"Military."

"What rank?"

" Colonel."

" Your name ? "

" Alexandre de Lameth."

Upon which the young Frenchman looks fixedly at his general, and replies :

" What nationality are you ? "

" Russian, apparently."

" What profession ? "

" Military."

" What rank ? "

" General."

" Your name ? "

" Suvorof."

The future vanquisher of Macdonald was quite capable of giving and taking an interrogation of this kind. The future commandant of a division of Condé's army, Roger de Damas, *Damaderoger*, as Patiomkin, in the Russian manner, generally called him, made his appearance about the same time at the head-quarters of the conqueror of the Crimea. The nephew of the Duc de Châtelet, whose diplomatic disagreements with one of the Tshernishofs we have already related, he brought with him somewhat embarrassing recollections. According to Langeron, however, the former ambassador of Catherine showed no ill-will to the nephew on his uncle's account, and, indeed, amused himself by recalling the fact that he had had occasion of seeing the latter at very close quarters in London, which, in a sense, was the exact truth.

Damaderoger is the delight and astonishment of the Russian army. He learns Russian in a few months,

and, under the walls of Otchakof, wins a sword of
honour which Patiomkin demands for him, and Catherine hastens to send with a flattering inscription
engraved upon it. He mounts the walls in twenty-four
degrees of cold, "dressed as if he were going to the
ball," is one of the first to enter the fortress, and, on his
return, finds his French servant waiting for him with
his cloak. Almost at the same time another Frenchman,
Lombard, put in command of a frigate, distinguishes
himself by passing right through the Turkish fleet, and,
on being made prisoner in another engagement, is so
deeply regretted by Catherine, that she begs Ségur and
Choiseul-Gouffier to endeavour "to get him exchanged
at no matter what price."

At the siege of Bender in 1789, under the walls of
Ismaïl in 1790, there are not less than a dozen Frenchmen, the Duc de Richelieu, the Comte de Verbois, the
Comte de Langeron, the Chevalier de Vilnau, Rosset,
all equally brave and joyous, all doing honour to the
fatherland which they have left. Vilnau, under-lieu-
tenant in the French army, but obliged to fly after
killing his colonel in a duel, and now captain of light
cavalry in the Russian army, is always in the front
rank. At Bender he offers himself for the task of setting
the petard which is to blow up one of the gates of the
fortress, risks an almost certain death, survives his in-
juries by a sort of miracle, and, when he is invalided,
receives the post of governor of Her Majesty's pages.
On the eve of the taking of Ismaïl, those who are still
able to be under arms sit down to supper together gaily,
spend the night in playing cards, and in all kinds of

follies, and, at the moment of parting, calculating that
a third of the assailants will probably be left on the field
of battle, draw lots to see who will be the four to be
killed. They are all fortunate enough to escape with
only a few slight wounds. The Duc de Richelieu has
his hat shot through, one of his boots torn open, and his
trousers cut into bits. Verbois, later on, is killed in the
Black Sea, on one of the Prince of Nassau's ships, during
the Swedish war.

At the further bounds of the empire the Swedish
war brings to the front a number of recruits from the
same source. The Comte de Langeron, who, later on,
returning to the forgotten traditions of mercenary
loyalism, is unscrupulous enough to take advantage
of his engagement as *condottiere*, to the extent of com-
manding a corps of the Russian army under the very
walls of Paris, but in whom there was then, after his
campaign in America under Rochambeau, nothing to
arouse any such suspicions, does full justice in Finland
to his reputation for skill and bravery. His unpublished
memoirs, from which we have drawn largely, remain an
invaluable document for the history of the time. Prévôt
de Launion, a mere captain of artillery, improvises some
admirable tactics for the closure of the water-ways in
Finland. The naval captain, De Traversay, who succeeds to Verbois, attains the rank of rear-admiral, and
becomes the father of a warlike race now firmly
established in Russia. The regiment of dragoons,
stationed for some years past at Kalisz, on the German
frontier, has for colonel a descendant of the brave
sea-captain.

On April 8, 1791, Génet writes from St. Petersburg to the Comte de Montmorin :

" On Monday the Empress distributed the laurels of the last war : M. de Richelieu is to have a sword of gold and the Cross of St. George of the fourth class ; M. de Damas the cross of the third class. M. de Langeron will have a sword of gold, and will be appointed colonel in the Russian army according to his seniority in the French army."

It is not only the Comte de Ségur, however, who gives a helping hand, and doubtless not without a substantial return for the favour, to this influx of volunteers ; but La Harpe, too, Swiss as he is and Republican as he pretends to be. A curious chapter could be written on the part played at St. Petersburg by this enthusiastic disciple of Locke and Rousseau, this pontiff of liberty and rationalism, this admirer of Brutus and despiser of Cæsar, who sets up Julian the Apostate and depreciates Constantine the Great, keeping up an active correspondence with the worst demagogues of his country and acting as tutor to the future founder of the Holy Alliance. The secret of Catherine's approval of this education, which she defends against frequent onslaughts, is the secret of her own conscience and her innermost thoughts. With all his revolutionary notions and connections, La Harpe seems to her neither odious nor dangerous, because she has no fear of any such revolution at St. Petersburg, and because, at bottom, she sympathizes with the greater part of the principles which lie at the root of this new movement which is now beginning to agitate Europe. What the man may do or encourage

in France or Switzerland is a matter of perfect indifference to her ; it is no concern of hers ; and as for what
he says or writes, she could almost say it after him, at
all events at the beginning of the new crisis. Later on,
associated with the anti-revolutionary campaign by
reasons of political strategy, in which she has no personal
feeling, she comes gradually to admit a certain personal
feeling into the matter. But, in 1791, Génet still seems
to dread, in her, very different sentiments, as we see
from his dispatch of the 14th of June of that year,
referring to the arrival at Paris of the Comte de Sombreuil, who is supposed to be the bearer of a commission
from the French anti-revolutionaries :

" It is true that this princess, by reason of the constitution of her empire, cannot but manifest very different
principles from those which serve as base to our new
constitution, but I venture to assure you, Monsieur, that
the genius which has dictated the sublime ' instructions '
in regard to the laws, which has shown such encouragement towards the writers to whom we owe the progress
of enlightenment and the stamping out of fanaticism,
which has devised for Russia a philosophic code worthy
of the admiration of all the ages, will enter neither
directly nor indirectly into the mad projects of those
who, unfortunately for themselves, have endeavoured to
sow discord in a people which is engaged, in concert
with its monarch, in the grandest political enterprise
which any society has ever undertaken."

The passage is unmistakable enough, and it is a
special pleading, addressed rather to the sovereign herself than to the minister, but it is singularly true. And,

at bottom, even in her most furious tirades against Jacobinism, her most vehement declarations on behalf of the monarchical principle, Catherine does, in a certain sense, escape the reproach of self-contradiction and of apostasy to her philosophic past ; for what she objects to in the Revolution is not the principles on which that Revolution is based, but the use it has made of them. Might not these principles be carried out less violently and more wisely ?   Catherine professes that she herself has proved that they can.   What she has always dreamt of is a very despotic monarchy based on very liberal ideas.   She has not perhaps entirely succeeded in carrying out this programme ; but should not her grandson Alexander carry it out to its conclusion?   And so La Harpe is in his right place ; so it is that in 1791 and even in 1793 she resolutely retains him there, no matter what endeavours are made to arouse her apprehensions and scruples.   In 1791 the exiles of Coblenz induce Rumiantsof, who has been sent to them as ambassador, to denounce the relations of La Harpe with the agitators of the Vaudois canton.   She merely laughs with La Harpe over the charge.   In the following year, as certain other exiles are defending, before the whole court, the policy of the *ancien régime*, Alexander's brother, the Grand-Duke Constantine, a child of hardly thirteen, who is also a pupil of La Harpe, interrupts them :

" That is an entirely wrong account of things ! "

" Where did you get your information, Monseigneur ? "

" From the memoirs of Duclos, that I have read with La Harpe."

She laughs once more. In 1793, the presence of the
Comte d'Artois at St. Petersburg gives new force to
the attacks upon the supposed Jacobin tendencies
of the tutor. A compatriot of La Harpe who accompanies the prince, the Chevalier Roll, speaks on behalf
of the patriciate of Berne, uneasy on account of the
tutor's relations with his brother the general, who is
an ally of the Jacobins in Paris. Catherine merely gives
a gentle reminder to her *protégé* that he had better not
mix himself up with the affairs of his country. And
she gives him the opportunity of defending himself,
and even his principles, in a justificative memorial
which she herself puts in circulation.

Unfortunately for the tutor, and still more so for the
tuition, of Alexander, the excellent advice by which the
Empress had hoped to cut short the troublesome and
compromising relations in which he was concerned, has
an unexpected and disastrous effect : La Harpe lets
politics alone in Switzerland only to meddle with them
in Russia. Whatever some may have said on the subject, whatever he may have said himself, his banishment
is due entirely to this reason. He is seized with the
idea, which is anything but shared by Catherine, of a
reconciliation between Paul and his two sons ; which, he
conceives, will be an effectual obstacle to Catherine's
supposed intention of setting aside the succession to
the throne. This soon settles matters ! On December
27, 1793, a well-informed courtier writes from St. Petersburg to Prince Kurakin : " A certain M. Harpe, major
and chevalier of St. Vladimir, who held the post of tutor
to S. A. I. Mgr. the Grand-Duke Alexander, has been

arrested and sent across the frontier. The cause is supposed to have been the discovery of his Jacobinism. . . . These are the serpents that we warm in our bosoms ! "

This well-informed courtier, who is no other than Bantish-Kaminski, a high official in the bureau of Foreign Affairs, and the father of the writer of a popular dictionary of historical celebrities, is, for once, in the wrong : the Jacobinism of the Chevalier of St. Vladimir has nothing to do with the matter ; no more, indeed, than La Harpe, despite his own insinuations on the subject, had to do with the delay of the Russian armies in actually taking up arms against the Revolution.

The tutor is much regretted. " I don't want to read," declares young Constantine one day to his successor, Count Sacken ; " you are always reading, and you only get more stupid ! " La Harpe, on returning to France, finds himself in the wake of the revolutionary armies, and the principles which he then professes are much the same as those which, half unconsciously perhaps, he has professed even at St. Petersburg, under the indulgent eyes of Catherine herself. Appointed member of the directorate of the Swiss Republic, he manifests in the exercise of his functions precisely the ideal of govern ment dreamt of by the great sovereign : he is as despotic and as liberal as possible. He even plans another 18th Brumaire, of which he is to be the hero ; a project which only results in a hasty dismissal on the part of his fellow-citizens, and therewith the end of his political career.

III.

The arrival of the Comte de Saint-Priest at St. Petersburg in 1791 marks a new epoch in the history of the French colony established in Russia : that of emigration. From this moment, Catherine begins to pick and choose among the Frenchmen who recommend themselves to her favour, and, to succeed in that, it is necessary to have a clean record. The painter Doyen, who presents himself with a somewhat revolutionary past behind him, is at first sent about his business. " I did not see him," writes Catherine to Grimm, on the 9th of May, 1792, " for we do not admit Frenchmen so easily ; at least, not until they have gone through political quarantine." The ordeal is not, however, so very difficult, and Doyen ere long has passed successfully through it, and even achieved a very brilliant position at the court. But the emigrants do their best to heighten the rigour of the *consigne*. They come in shoals. Saint-Priest is required by the diplomatic body of Coblenz to obtain Catherine's aid in the expedition which the King of Sweden is thinking of undertaking in France, in order to re-establish order. He comes a little too soon, and meets with but a cold welcome. Introduced as he is by the official representative of constitutional monarchy against which he wishes the Empress to take up arms, he comes under dubious auspices, which are not likely to augment his chances. Later on, in September 1791, comes Esterhazy, sent by the Comte d'Artois to report the Pilnitz conferences to the Empress. He succeeds better, thanks to the personal charms which formerly won him the familiar friendship of Marie-Antoinette. He brings with him the prestige of the older Versailles. Once the page of King Stanislas, the *protégé* of Marie Leszczynska, he has still before him an honourable career in the French army. The mother of Marie-Antoinette has refused to allow his return to Austria, on account of his dissolute life ; but the scruples of " Saint Theresa " are not likely to have much influence on the mind of Saint Catherine. Esterhazy also finds means to ingratiate himself with the favourite Zubof, who takes him unceremoniously to the Hermitage, brings him through room after room, and then, opening a door, pushes him in, saying, " There she is ! " Brought thus into *tête-à-tête* with the sovereign, he does not lose his presence of mind, and succeeds in making an agreeable impression. Catherine listens inattentively to his diplomatic communications, but she offers to take him into her service and supply all his wants, and that is precisely what he is aiming at. After the final fall of the Bourbons, he lives quietly on the estates that she gives him in Volhynia.

Sombreuil, too, at about the same time, comes to take up his abode in Russia, and is received as aide-de-camp by the Prince de Nassau. He has many imitators. " MM. de Fürstemberg, de Schweizer, de Lambert, and de Vendre," writes Génet in April 1791, "have asked permission to be admitted as volunteers in the Russian army . . . all received higher rank than they had in France, and are treated with distinction at the court." Two months before the attempt of Varennes, the Marquis de Bouillé himself offers his services to the Empress of

Russia, through Grimm. General Heymann, a brilliant cavalry officer, whom he sends to Paris to set matters on foot, intends to follow in his footsteps. There is some disagreement as to conditions, for Catherine replies curtly that her generals cost less and are worth quite as much as the French. But Grimm soon has other propositions to make: a Vioménil and a Vauban wish "to devote themselves to the service of a sovereign who has taken victory into her pay"; a young Prince de Craon burns to betake himself to Russia, in order to "pay his first devotions in the temple of glory"; a Marquis de Juigné, head of a large family, and deprived by the Revolution of the means of providing for them, "desires to forget his troubles by donning the uniform of Her Imperial Majesty." Others come straight to St. Petersburg: in September 1791 Génet announces the arrival of MM. de Boisgelin, de Fortin, and de Veuzotte. Soon it is the whole army, or at least the remains of it, Condé at its head, with 1500 men still under its flag, that demands shelter in the ranks of the Imperial army. But Catherine has soldiers enough. In December 1792, Richelieu, the hero of Ismaïl, arrives at the head-quarters of Condé with two sledges containing 60,000 roubles in silver and a letter from the Empress offering the emigrants—a settlement on the eastern shore of the sea of Azof, a city to found in a desert! She has already allotted the ground, and drawn up the plan of the houses to be built. Richelieu is to be governor, Esterhazy inspector of works, and Condé general inspector, in this distant land, behind the Kouban, with about 300,000 francs as capital! The consternation of the unhappy

G

waifs of fortune can easily be imagined : " We would
sooner die," writes one of them.

Just then Catherine was anxious to make a great
show, and do little, on the Rhine ; and the appearance
of Richelieu in the camp of Condé with his barrels of
money and his very unattractive proposals, was probably
done for this purpose. Rumiantsof had been there for
the last two years, passing in review this army of
gentlemen, solemnly haranguing the Maréchal de Broglie,
but, in point of fact, doing nothing beyond becoming
the favourite of the platonic favourite of Monsieur.
Nassau, in full uniform as Russian admiral, also figured
there, keeping open house, heaping feast on feast and
enthusiastic toast on toast. Catherine intervened from
time to time, with a little in the way of aid and a great
deal in the way of counsel, not always easy to follow,
as when she advised the princes never to receive any
one in evening dress, so as to " dismiss the idea of
equality." Alas ! the poor princes were in danger of
soon seeing about them people who had not so much as
a dress suit to put on. She wished it all to be taken
seriously, and, serious herself in her resolve to do nothing
which should be so, she all but succeeded, Monsieur,
in spite of all his disappointments, being unable to
compare her to anything but Prometheus " stealing fire
from heaven to warm the earth."

A regiment of 1500 Frenchmen in her pay would
have been of little use to her, but it pleased her to have
a Richelieu under the orders of her generals, as it did
also to people her salons with the flower of the chief
nobility of Europe. " Madame Vigée-Lebrun will soon

imagine that she is in Paris, so many Frenchmen are
at all the parties here," wrote the Prince de Ligne in
1793 in a sketch of St. Petersburg society. She lodged
Esterhazy in her palace, gave a pension to Bombelles,
employed Saint-Priest in certain diplomatic missions,
and gave a hearty welcome to Choiseul-Gouffier, whose
rôle of peace-maker at Constantinople had commended
him to her. She even decided him to take up his
abode in her empire, and thus made capture of one
noble lineage the more, of which France has since
recaptured certain branches. There is even a family
legend to the effect that the sovereign had, at first,
a more tender interest in the former ambassador, and
that his austere virtue led him to act the part of Joseph
in a scene very humiliating for Semiramis. It is forgotten
that, born in 1752, Choiseul had long passed the age of
Plato and Valerian Zubof, and the amorous fancies of
Catherine have no need of calling in the miracle of the
multiplying. But it is natural that the imagination of
contemporaries should have ranged freely on such a
subject, and that people should have seen double, and
triple, in regard to a romance which, without that, was
quite sufficiently varied.

Semiramis also gave some encouragement to the
society poet Grimaut, to the tactician Tranchant de
Laverne, the future author of two indifferent biographies
of Patiomkin and Suvorof. She even so far forgot her
prejudices against the painter Doyen as to give him a
place in the theatre near her own box. She appointed
him decorator of her palace and professor in her
Academy, though she knew well that in Paris he had

drawn up the inventory of the works of art confiscated from the convents.

Local society could not but follow in the steps of the Empress, and all vied with one another in receiving the greatest number of the refugees, and paying them the greatest attentions. The salon of Madame Divof is known as " Little Coblenz " ; it is the head-quarters of wit *à la française*, sometimes at the Empress's expense. A libel which circulates there is recognized as the work of a refugee in the Empress's pension. At the Princess Dolgoruki's, Catherine is censured by means of rhapsodies on the talent of Madame Vigée-Lebrun. At Prince Bielossielski's, the French verses of the master of the house, which, as we know, Catherine thought little enough of, are much admired. Everywhere there is love-making in the manner of both countries. In this respect, there is a confusion of customs, tastes, and passions of different order, more refined on the one side, more emphatic on the other, but with an equal licence on either side. It is Versailles planted bodily down at St. Petersburg.

From this accidental fusion of two heterogeneous elements, something more has come about than the mingling of two kinds of corruption. If Gogol, the author of *Dead Souls*, has seen in it only the perversion of the national genius by puerilities proper to the French temperament, Turguenief has traced, even in the most out-of-the-way nooks and corners, the profound and significant penetration of quite other and much more serious ideas, inspirations, and tendencies of similar origin. Now, it is not the spirit of the old

French monarchy, nor that of an impotent reaction
against the revolutionary movement, which thus pene-
trates to the very heart of ancient Moscow. No, that
is confined to the drawing-rooms of the capital ; outside, it is something quite different which this crowd of
strangers disseminates around it.   For, though these
refugees are the victims or the adversaries of the Revolution, they are also its issue.   They have been carried
by the flood ; some of them have helped it onward, and,
despite themselves, they bear its influence, they communicate its movement.   The ideas, inspirations, and
tendencies which Turguenief has traced, are indeed
those which have created modern France.

Certainly they are slow in making progress in these
surroundings, so little prepared to receive them ; they
may almost be said to remain in the air like the frozen
words of a local legend, which cannot be heard till the
return of spring.   But they are there, they wait their
time, and when once they feel the regenerating breezes
of April, they will wake to life.   The great work of libera-
tion, in 1861, comes in part from this, without doubt.

Catherine is doubtless in ignorance of the distant
future of this indirect propaganda, or sees it too far in
the future to be concerned about it.   She tolerates even
the meetings of the Café Henri, a sort of club where
people go to drink punch and talk politics, and where
very free discussions are held in French.   This association of refugees, assisting unwittingly in the carrying
out of a task whose accomplishment will not be seen for
several generations, strikes her especially, as it has since
struck Gogol, by its mask of frivolity, which at once

amuses and reassures her, at the same time that it distresses certain morose observers, who do not share in the general enthusiasm. Seeing the gestures, and not hearing a word—the sound suspended for the moment in this freezing atmosphere—these serious persons find the pantomime exaggerated and ridiculous. " I am surprised," writes the Count Rastoptshin, " that these people can inspire any interest. I have never found any other in them than that .which one finds in the performance of a moving drama, for this nation exists only by and in its acting. When one studies the French, one finds something so volatile in their whole being, that one cannot conceive how they manage to keep to the earth. The scoundrels and idiots have remained in their own country, and the madmen have quitted it to increase the number of charlatans in the world."

Catherine too acts a comedy, cheaply enough, with these mainly eminent representatives of a world about to disappear. The arrival of the Comte d'Artois in 1793 enchants her: it is a splendid bit of spectacular effect. She had dreamt for a moment, before Varennes, of giving hospitality to Louis XVI. himself. She had declared that it would be " the most remarkable act of her reign." A Princess of Zerbst giving shelter to the grandson of St. Louis: she knew what that would mean ! She keeps for a whole month the son of France that she has the good luck to have in her hands, and tries upon him all the pomps of her court and all the charms of her person. He behaves very properly on his side ; " admirable," declares Langeron, " simple, decent, modest, and sincerely distressed, without swagger or affectation, manifesting in his conversation a cold and sane judgment, contradicting all the notions general in Russia in regard to his frivolity and youthful gaieties, inspiring the most lively and respectful interest." But he does not succeed in engaging Catherine in a single conversation in which the affairs of the refugees and the question of royalty were seriously considered. Catherine was a past master in the art of evasion. He gets on better with Zubof, who, more flattered still, is prodigal at all events of promises.

At the end of a month, Semiramis seems to have exhausted her resources. The prince's companions are not very agreeable either. The Bishop of Arras has "too much the manner and language of a grenadier." The Chevalier Roll gets too much entangled in the affairs of Switzerland and La Harpe. The Comte d'Escars does not find the Empress's table worthy of so great an Empress, and makes no disguise of his opinion. The parting hour has struck. The prince sets out with the favourite's promises, which nearly bring him to a debtor's prison in England, with a little money on which he lives for a short time in Germany, and with the famous sword, "given by God to the king," which, in the following year, at Hamm, passes into the hands of an usurer in order to pay for the toilet of Madame de Polastron. "I should not give it to you," Catherine had said to him in solemn audience, "if I were not persuaded that you would perish sooner than postpone using it." He uses it, poor prince, in the only way he knows how to.

Calonne, who comes after, fares worse. Catherine is accustomed to look upon the French within her borders, not as guests, but as new subjects, and she will not hear of their giving themselves airs. The former controller-general gives her the impression, too, of a mischief-maker. Besides, she is gradually outgrowing her spirit of professed tolerance, at the outset of the revolutionary crisis, towards the conflict of ideas and principles to which it gave rise. She has gradually come to believe in the sentiments that she has so long professed outwardly to her German neighbours, without in any way believing them. She is not yet inclined to set out for the re-establishment of throne and altar in France, but she feels the impulse to hit out at those Frenchmen whom she has at hand. In 1795 it is not only the drawing-room of St. Petersburg in which Calonne's compatriots are to be seen, but the prisons as well. Bonneau, ex-consul-general of France at Warsaw, has been there for the past two years. An order of Sievers, the all-powerful representative of Catherine on the banks of the Vistula, has one night arrested him and hurried him away without trial to St. Petersburg. His neighbour, in the prison of St. Peter and St. Paul, is a compatriot who has been put there on account of some irregularity in his passport. The latter goes mad at the end of six months, is sent to a hospital, cured, sent back to prison, and this time becomes raving mad. When he makes too much noise he is beaten with rods until he is quiet. Kosciuszko and his aide-de-camp know him, and find means of communicating with him : he is twenty-five years of age, and is called Forges. And neither Voltaire nor D'Alembert is there to interfere in his favour! The friend of the philosophers is equally absent: it is Catherine II. who reigns now, and who is soon to attempt the imprisonment of France itself under the guard of 60,000 jailers whom Suvorof is ready to lead there.

CHAPTER V.

ADVENTURERS AND ADVENTURESSES.—PRINCESS TARAKANOF.

I.

To call up the picture of a court of the eighteenth century, and not to assign their place to a certain number of adventurers, would be too obvious an act of forgetfulness. Catherine does not escape the common destiny: the Piedmontese Odart figures among her familiars from 1762 onwards. He disappears after the *coup d'État*, returns some years afterwards, this time in order to conspire against the widow of Peter III., and then disappears finally, killed, it is supposed, by a thunderbolt at Nice. But he leaves others of his kind at St. Petersburg, for in 1788 Langeron comes across an Italian who is so like him as to be taken for him. He calls himself the Count Morelli, his real name being Rosatti, a former bandsman in a French regiment. His voice, his guitar, and no doubt some other talents, have given him access to Prince Patiomkin. When the second Turkish war breaks out, he is Count, Colonel, and Knight of St. George. Langeron, who has just arrived in Russia, with an honourable and glorious past, waits in vain for a commission which he has been led to anticipate in regard to the Austrian army. He is in despair, when Rosatti, or Count Morelli, gives him to understand that his only chance of obtaining employment is by paying a visit to M. Altesti. This is an Illyrian adventurer, secretary of the favourite Zubof, and second minister, specially charged with the employment or surveillance of the strangers in Russia. After some hesitation Langeron consents: "His ante-room," he relates, "from seven in the morning, was as crowded as that of Zubof . . . I went to see him after dinner, found him, stayed in his salon for five minutes, and never mentioned the matter to him at all. Three days after I received my commission."

We have already had occasion to cite the sonorous name of another adventurer whom Betzki put in charge of the Beaux-Arts and the Corps des Cadets. This pseudo-Lascaris is also an Italian, the son of a Neapolitan named Carburi, who deals in spices in the Isle of Cephalonia. His imposture and real origin are one day exposed by the wife of a consul of Ragusa, a true Lascaris, who comes to St. Petersburg. It makes no difference ; but soon after he is expelled from the Corps des Cadets on account of a shameful charge brought against him by the chaplain of the establishment. Employment is then found for him in the police.

In 1764 a brother of Baron François de Tott, the Hungarian whose diplomatic and military career in the service of France had been so meritorious, appears at St. Petersburg. He accompanies Madame Saltykof, the

wife of the Russian minister at Paris, who has to return
to her native country on account of her health.   He is
soon at home in the best society of the capital, serves as
volunteer in the "camp" of thirty thousand men then
gathered at Tsarskoïe, shares the tent of the favourite
Orlof, and is presented by him to the Empress.   Unluckily, he gets into debt, and thereupon endeavours to
make use of his brilliant social relations and the French
cavalry uniform that he bears, no one knows why or
wherefore, by offering his services to Bausset, the French
envoy then in office.   Just then Bausset dies, and he
dreams for a moment of taking his place as *chargé
d'affaires*, then resigns himself to the less glorious post of
informer in the pay of the Legation.   On the strength of
his intimacy with Count Panin, he obtains the promise
of a high salary and the payment of his debts, but
Catherine's prime minister suspects what is going on,
and, in a friendly manner, advises the vendor of the
secrets of state to cross the frontier as speedily as
possible.   He even contributes towards the expenses
of this precipitate departure.   In a justification presented in 1771 to the Duc d'Aiguillon, de Tott excuses
himself, amusingly enough, from the unjust suspicion of
having been influenced by motives of personal interest:
" Set down a Russian at the court of France, with
common-sense, a name, good manners, in company with
the prime minister, in relations with the nobility of
both sexes ; suppose in him little fondness *pour ses
glaces (sic)* ; let him have eight thousand francs of debt,
and imagine whether or not he will get into embarrassed circumstances."

II.

The " Star of the North " would have failed to justify her name if her European lustre had not attracted the greatest adventurer of the time. Cagliostro takes several months to prepare a sensational entry on one of the most conspicuous stages of Europe in the latter half of the eighteenth century. Reaching Mittau in February 1779, he prolongs his stay there, watching and preparing his public, getting his scenery in order. He attributes to himself an important mission on behalf of the masonic order of which he is called upon to become the representative in the North. Eagerly welcomed in the Courland house of Count Medem, his appearance loudly trumpeted, he finds himself, on his arrival at St. Petersburg, in possession of all his customary means of action. Patiomkin, then at the outset of his favour, goes to see him, and has his reasons for going again, reasons to which the fair and fascinating Lorenza, who then goes under the name of the Princess of Santa Croce, is no stranger. According to one of the thousand reports which were then in circulation, Catherine herself intervenes in order to get rid of this rival, offering her thirty thousand roubles, which the lady refuses in favour of twice the amount on the part of the favourite. The story is highly improbable. Catherine had better means than that of getting rid of her rivals, and she has given too amusing an account, in a letter to Grimm, of the prowesses of the charlatan in her capital :

" He came here calling himself a colonel in the service

of Spain, and Spanish by birth, pretending to be a sorcerer, having spirits at his beck and call. When I heard that, I said : ' This man has made a great mistake in coming here ; nowhere will he succeed so badly as in Russia.' We do not burn sorcerers here, and for twenty years there has only been one single affair in which there were supposed to be any sorcerers, and then the Senate asked to see them, and, when they had been summoned, they were found to be quite stupid and perfectly innocent. M. Cagliostro, however, has come just at the right moment for himself, when several lodges of freemasons, which had taken up Swedenborg's principles, were anxious at all costs to see spirits ; they therefore ran to Cagliostro, who declared he had all the secrets of Doctor Falk, an intimate friend of the Duc de Richelieu, and who formerly sacrificed to the black goat in the midst of Vienna . . . M. Cagliostro then produced his marvellous cures ; he pretended to extract quicksilver from a gouty man's leg, and he was taken in the act of pouring a teaspoonful of quicksilver into the water in which he put the gouty man. Then he produced dyes which would dye nothing, and chemical preparations which would not work . . . After which, it has been discovered that he could hardly read or write. Finally, overwhelmed with debts, he took refuge in the cellar of M. Ielaguine, where he drank as much champagne and English beer as he could. One day apparently he exceeded the usual measure, for, on leaving his repast, he hooked himself on to the wig of the secretary of the house, who boxed his ears, whereupon there was a free fight ; M. Ielaguine, tired alike of his cellar-rat and of the expenditure of wine and beer, as well as of his secretary's complaints, politely persuaded him to take his departure in a *kibitka*, and not in the air, as he threatened, and in order that his creditors should put no hindrance in the way of this brisk means of conveyance, he gave him an old soldier to accompany him and Madame la Comtesse as far as Mittau. There is the whole story of Cagliostro, in which there is everything but the marvellous. I never saw him, even at a distance, nor had any inclination to."

The Princess of Santa Croce, or, more simply, Madame Cagliostro, seems to have had no share, after all, in the failure of this expedition. Catherine always had, as we know, an exceptional allowance for the amorous caprices of the most capricious and amorous of her favourites. Some years before, the future Prince of Taurida had sighed after the charms, already somewhat faded, of another foreign visitor of more or less the same category, and Catherine had not appeared to be jealous in the least. She even found the fair charmer intelligent, and she was not often given to such kinds of compliment. This was the famous Duchess of Kingston, widow of the duke of that name, but the undivorced wife of a first husband still living, a Captain Hervey; so that she added bigamy to the other gallant adventures which she had had under her maiden name of Elizabeth Chudleigh, once maid-of-honour of the Princess of Wales. She comes to St. Petersburg in 1777, with a numerous following, and an almoner, Abbé Séchamp. She is presented to the Empress under the title which is disputed in England, she is supposed even to belong to the royal family, is invited to Tsarskoïe-Sielo, and meets with the most flattering reception. She gives balls to which everybody in St. Petersburg comes, both on board her yacht, whose luxurious fittings cause universal admiration, and in her house, one of the finest in the city, which is put at her disposal by the Empress. The yacht having been somewhat damaged in a storm, Catherine has it set right at her own expense. The adventuress is cunning enough to tell every one that she has come simply and solely to have the delight and honour of seeing the most extraordinary woman of the past and present times, and Semiramis likes to hear it said. Patiomkin openly pays court to the pseudo-duchess, and Catherine lets him do it. It should be said that this new rival is fifty-seven years of age, and is beginning to be deaf, and she also appears to take special interest in one of the favourite's secretaries, Garnovski, who comes later to appropriate a part of her large fortune. For, wishing to push her claims, she begins to dream of gaining official standing at the court, and buys an estate in Esthonia. But unfavourable rumours begin to be circulated on her account, and she thinks it best to go into retirement for a time ; and when, in 1782, she returns, it is all up: no one will have anything to do with her, at the court or elsewhere, the favourite turns his back on her, and Garnovski, in whom she has placed all her confidence, takes advantage of it to lay hands on her Esthonian estate,

III.

Two years before the first appearance of this adventuress, the fortress of St. Peter and Paul had seen the end of the romance of another woman, adventurous in quite another way, mysterious also, and whom it is almost a little painful to bring into this chapter, so much of melancholy and pitiful interest is there in a story which suits so ill with the more ordinary vulgarity of this kind of episode. All is mystery in this singular figure, so phantom-like, a mystery which even rumour has been unable to enlighten. She lived and died surrounded with mystery, and, apart from the misty circle of more or less imaginary facts which are reported about her, it is scarcely possible to-day to really reconstruct her personal identity or her place in history.

Her name? She has none. In the legend, and even in what history there is, she commonly bears the name of Princess Tarakanof. Now, not only is this not her true name, but it does not even appear that she herself ever thought of appropriating it, among all the masks which she donned. No Princess Tarakanof, true or false, has ever had a moment's existence. Legend and history have come upon a false track, making the name of Tarakanof out of Daragan, the name of one of Razumovski's nephews; but while there are Daragans still occupying high positions in Russia, there never has been a Tarakanof, either in the fortress of St. Peter and Paul, or anywhere else.

Her civil state? She has none. She passes for a

daughter of Elizabeth and Razumovski. Hence the confusion with the Daragans. In prison, under torture, in the last agonies, she obstinately denies having wished to usurp this title. Could she do so with any show of truth ? Was there any offspring of the marriage of Elizabeth with the chorister of Little Russia ? There is doubt on this point also.

One supposed certainty has for a long time stood out from so many insoluble enigmas. In 1864 at St. Petersburg, and three years later at Paris, a picture by the Russian painter, Flavintski, drew crowds of spectators by a terrifying representation of the death of a young and beautiful woman, imprisoned in a vault of the fortress of Schlüsselburg, surprised by the sudden rising of the Neva, and drowned in her cell. It was imagined to be a historical picture of the death of the supposed Princess Tarakanof. Well, after all, there is nothing historical in this dismal exhibition. A careful investigation has established these facts : that the inundation represented by the painter took place in 1777, at which time the supposed Princess Tarakanof had been dead two years, and she was never imprisoned at Schlüsselburg at all.

Who is she, then, this nameless being, whose sombre destiny has distracted the imagination of artists and put to task the knowledge of historians ? Who did she even profess to be ? What part was it that she wished to play ? Still mystery ! Not by a word has she ever unveiled the secret of her conscience. Was she ever conscious of it herself ? Did she herself know what we are so anxious to know about her ? Among those who were passionately desirous of penetrating her secret was the Duke of Limburg. All the reply that he received in answer to his pressing and imperious questions is this dubious one: "You ask me for the truth? You would never believe me if I told it to you. And, then, what is truth? What is falsehood? In this strange comedy of life which we are obliged to act out, and in which we are not allowed to choose our part, are you able to distinguish between the mask and the face which it covers? To deceive ourselves and one another is the common lot of all. We all lie. Only, some do it without method or design, and are lost by the way, while others fancy that they know their way and make straight for the goal, lying always, but lying systematically. I would be of those."

The first appearance of this enigmatic actress took place at Paris in 1772. People notice a Princess Aly Emettée de Vlodomir, a name strangely made up of Sclavonic and Persian sounds, coming from no one knows where. She is young and fair, gracious of aspect, with blonde hair like that of Elizabeth, and eyes changing colour like hers, now blue, now black, which give to her face that air of strangeness and dreaminess which has always clung about her person and her destiny. Her manners are admirable, and she seems to have received a most careful education. She gives herself out for a Tcherkess, the niece of an immensely rich Persian lord. She has a numerous suite, among which are two Germans; a Baron von Embs, who plays the part of a middle-aged relative, and a Baron von Schenk, who unites the office of intendant with that of confi-

dential friend.   The princess lives in great style, and
is soon in possession of a very wide circle of acquaintances.   The strangers who are then so frequent in Paris
are to be seen at her house, together with a certain
number of Frenchmen.   The Polish refugees, who are
just then beginning to arrive, furnish a considerable
and illustrious contingent to her salon.   Prince Michael
Oginski, one of the most conspicuous of these exiles,
is seen among the admirers of the fair Tcherkess.   Suddenly there is a catastrophe : the respectable middle-
aged relation is arrested for debt, and it is discovered
that he has no right to the name and title which he
bears.   He is no baron, and his real name is that of
a rich merchant of Ghent, towards whom he has long
played the part of prodigal son.   The news spreads,
and there is naturally a rush of creditors to the luxurious abode of the princess ; but another surprise awaits
them : the house is empty, the princess is gone.

A few months afterwards she re-appears at Frankfort,
always accompanied by a number of servants, staying
in the best lodgings in the town, and treated with the
greatest respect.   Her Parisian tradesmen are not long
in following on her track ; but a saviour presents himself,
the Duke of Limburg, himself deeply in debt, but having
subjects whom he still has means of making use of ; he
generously offers to relieve the princess of her embar-
rassments, and finally instals her in his castle of Oberstein.   He expects, naturally, the reward of his chivalry ;
but the princess is not to be taken.   He then goes to
the point of offering her his hand in marriage ; it will
be no *mésalliance*, for she too has a sovereignty to give

him: she has changed her name and origin, it is the Princess of Azov, a scion of the princely house of Vlodimir, and heiress of a principality under the protectorate of Russia, who is to become Duchess of Limburg.

Up to now the adventure is a commonplace one, like a hundred others of the period. False barons and princesses swarm in the capitals and even in the small towns. The greater rapidity of communications and the much more certain division of social conditions are even now scarcely enough to bar their way. In the eighteenth century, when there was no telegraph, when the *Almanach de Gotha* had only begun to appear in 1764, and geographical and ethnological knowledge was but at its commencement, the existence of principalities of Azov under the protection of Russia was not easy to inquire into. Even in our own day such things are not always found out in time. In 1772, at the castle of Oberstein, the future Duchess of Limburg could well find elbow-room. A moment comes, however, when the Duke's purse grows so desperately empty, and the subsidies which the Princess of Azov is expecting from her principalities are so long in coming, that relations between the *fiancés* become strained, and the confidence which has reigned till then begins to waver. But by this time the Duke of Limburg has already a successor, and it is now that the romance of the fair unknown takes a turn which carries it out of trivial issues into the domain of history.

The castle of Oberstein is near Mannheim, where for some months another Polish exile, more illustrious still

than Prince Oginski, Prince Radziwill, has been living ;
the Prince Radziwill whom a legend, entirely without
foundation, represents carrying over Europe twelve life-
size statues of the Apostles in solid gold, which he has
succeeded in rescuing from his castle at Nieswiez when
it was pillaged by the Russians, and which serve pro-
visionally to cover his travelling expenses. The Princess
of Azov hears of her neighbour, and is not slow to turn
her fair tearful eyes in his direction. Despite the absence
of the twelve imaginary Apostles, the great Polish lord,
who still retains more definite fragments of a royal
fortune, is a highly desirable catch. But he is suspicious
and eccentric, and feminine charms have little power
over him. No matter ! The great actress who has not
told her secret to the Duke of Limburg has other means
of seduction besides the enigmatic charm of her changing
eyes. A sudden shift of scenery brings her out in a
new light. There is no longer a Princess of Azov ; there
is no longer a principality of Vlodimir ; there is only a
nameless orphan, or rather one with so lofty a name
that it can only be whispered, and that under mortal
peril. Brought up in a convent, then banished to Siberia,
she has been liberated by her prison-warders, and taken
to Persia. Nevertheless, in all her wanderings, she has
preserved a coffer in which is deposited a document
which is at once her certificate of birth and her fortune.
It is worth an empire : it is the will of Elizabeth I.,
Empress of Russia, bequeathing her crown to Elizabeth
II., only issue of her marriage with Razumovski, and
Elizabeth II. is the mysterious châtelaine of Oberstein.

More or less documented pretenders, hypothetical

sons and daughters of kings and empresses, are no rarity in the eighteenth century, though the time of the Naundorffs is not yet come. But no matter! Radziwill's imagination is fired at once by the telling of this marvellous tale. He is just then dreaming of some bold attempt at recovering the liberty of his country. He dreams of making his way to Turkey, and demanding the aid of Ottoman arms. What an invaluable support to him in this expedition will be the simultaneous appearance in the Turko-Polish camp of the granddaughter of Peter the Great. She asks for nothing better; she will follow the exiled noble to Venice, where he is to put the finishing touch to his plans, and then to Constantinople.

And now the sentiments of the Duke of Limburg himself, greatly as they have cooled down, are requickened by the contact of this new brazier which his enigmatic friend has set on fire. Jealousy, ambition, all that is left of love, urge him on to new sacrifices. His subjects are bled to the last point, and it is with a train worthy of her rank that the daughter of Elizabeth reaches Venice, in March 1774. There is no question of marriage with the Duke. The future Empress of all the Russias could not condescend so far. Some months pass in feverish preparations and in *fêtes*; then the heiress of the Tsars goes before her new compatriots to Ragusa, where the embarkment is to take place. At the moment of parting she is publicly hailed as the legitimate sovereign of the great empire, and, as such, she solemnly renews the promises that she has already made to the Polish exiles.

At Ragusa the *rôle* thus assumed by the ex-princess of Azov is yet more brilliantly played. At Radziwill's request, the French consul, Descrivaux, gives up to her his own house, a delicious villa surrounded with gardens and vineyards. This charming abode becomes a popular centre, as also does the head-quarters of the little army waiting the moment to set sail for Constantinople. The august rank claimed by the adventuress gains a certain consistency, and she proclaims it by a decisive action : she writes to Alexis Orlof, who is at Leghorn with his squadron. There are rumours that the latter is about to make common cause with his brother, the favourite, who has lately fallen into disgrace. A copy of the testament of Elizabeth I. is sent him, with a ukase signed by Elizabeth II., which instructs him to communicate to the troops under his orders the last will of the daughter of the great Tsar.

One would suppose that *le Balafré* would shrug his shoulders at the joke, and the widow of Peter III. would merely laugh at it. By no means. Alexis Orlof refers the matter to Catherine, and she, in a letter dated November 12, 1774, bids the conqueror of Tchesmé, by force or by guile, and at all costs, seize upon the would-be grand-daughter of Peter I. If need be, he is to bombard Ragusa, and force the town to give her up. To bombard a town belonging to a state with which one is not at war is a serious affair ; evidently, therefore, the Empress must have looked upon the adventure, which she was so anxious to put an end to, as one of singular seriousness. As we have said, the would-be heiress of Elizabeth had a sufficient number of partners on the

look-out for European sovereignties, whom no one ever
thought of bombarding. And there is another significant
fact: eight years after these events, the Marquis de Vérac,
French minister at St. Petersburg, has the demand put
before him of a Sieur Marine, French subject, to
whom the Princess of Vlodomir owes a sum of fifty-two
thousand livres, dating from her sojourn of some
months at Paris, in 1772. The Marquis has never
heard of a princess of that name ; he makes inquiries,
and at the first word he is stopped : the princess is dead,
her creditors have been paid, and the Sieur Marine
would have been also if he had sent in his account.
The claim will be immediately settled. At this moment
certain French shipowners, who have been plundered by
Russian cruisers in the Mediterranean, are waiting in
vain for the indemnities which have been promised them
years before, and Catherine refuses to honour, even at
Paris, the debts of Bobrinski! Besides which, the
Marquis endeavours, privately if not officially, to obtain
further information in regard to the princess whose
existence he has been unaware of, and he comes to the
conclusion that it was really a daughter of the Empress
Elizabeth and Razumovski.

But to return to our story. *Le Balafré's* reply to
the communication made to him by the pretender is
naturally long in coming, and Elizabeth II. has not the
time to await it at Ragusa, where her affairs are getting
complicated. The treaty of Koutchouk-Kaïnardji (July
2, 1774) has put to rout the hopes of Radziwill and his
friends, and the voyage to Constantinople is abandoned.
Meanwhile, an awkward accident of a more private

character has done some damage to the situation of the grand-daughter of Peter I. While making the most of her personal charms, her youth and beauty, the princess had hitherto succeeded in keeping her reputation unblemished. She was supposed to be unattainable. Now one night a young knight in the suite of Radziwill, Domanski, is seen climbing over the wall of the Villa Descrivaux. A man on guard takes him for a robber, fires, and wounds him. There is a scandal, and Domanski's companions are somewhat disconcerted, especially as certain dubious rumours begin to reach them from Paris about the pretender.

As for her, she shows her usual decision by suddenly announcing her departure to Rome. Serious affairs calling her to the capital of the Christian world, where the problem of the succession of Clement XIV. is just beginning to be talked of, serve to cover her retreat. But, travelling now under the name of the Comtesse de Pimberg, she stops on the way at Naples, and there makes another conquest, that of Hamilton, the English envoy, the future husband of Emma Harte, who seems predestined to encounters of this sort. While listening, not too coldly, to the transports of the inflammable diplomatist, she prepares for her entry into the eternal city. Domanski, who has followed her with another Polish companion, Czarnomski, arranges the matter. At last she ventures thither, and, discreetly retired in a lonely palace on the left bank of the Tiber, apparently given over to good works, she is not long in winning great sympathy, as well as exciting a lively curiosity. Cardinal Albani, the protector of the Polish throne, manifests a respectful interest in her, and soon becomes enthusiastic himself as she confides in him her plans for the future and her vows of conversion, which open a dazzling vista before the piety and ambition of the Roman prelate. A Jesuit named Linday, who has formerly served in the Russian army, sees the new-comer, and declares that he recognizes in her the wife of a Duke of Oldenburg, whom he has visited at St. Petersburg. This only aids in confirming the legend which surrounds the mysterious princess. Unhappily her resources are exhausted. She ekes them out for a time by bartering diplomas of Limburg decor-ations and dignities, of which she has laid in an ample supply ; but at last, as the candidates for these honorary distinctions become rare, she has recourse to a last expedient : she appeals to the generosity of Hamilton. She writes him a letter, which is by no means whining, but, on the contrary, lofty, as if she were conferring a favour instead of asking for aid ; and in so doing she signs her own death-warrant : the man who is to con-duct her to prison and to death, and who has long been watching for his occasion, sees and seizes it now.

The sum required of Hamilton being a considerable one, he applies to his colleague at Leghorn, John Dick, English consul, and banker in that city. John Dick, who is on friendly terms with Alexis Orlof, informs the latter, who has just received peremptory orders from Catherine, which he now sees his way to carry out.

In eighteenth-century politics, nothing is more common than the laying of traps. The Russians only follow a universal and almost invariable custom. The German

Weickard relates in his memoirs the adventure, very ordinary in his eyes, of a Frenchman, whose name he does not know, who is captured at the Hague, by order of the Russian Government, taken to St. Petersburg, and shut up for life in the *oubliettes* of the Finnish fortress of Kexholm.

" He is a big scoundrel," declares the officer commissioned to carry out this proceeding, as he presents his capture to the Empress.

" You're a bigger, since you managed to catch him," replies Catherine.

In setting a trap, all means are good. There is a droll story concerning the famous Beniowsky, who has escaped from Kamschatka after having been sent there by the Russians, and who turns up at Spa in 1772 with the MS of a narrative of his Siberian odyssey, which he declares he is going to publish, and in which the Semiramis of the North is likely to be anything but amicably treated. A Russian agent is put on the track ; he secures the aid of a famous courtesan known as the *Ace of Spades*, on account of a beauty-spot, which she shows for a thaler. Poor Beniowsky sees the beauty-spot, but loses his MS.

The snare which is set for the Comtesse Pimberg is, in its kind, an unusually artistic one, a masterpiece of ingenuity and infamy. It is curious to see an Englishman and a Russian acting in concert, and both seeming to be equally devoid of scruples or of feelings of honour or pity. Alexis Orlof and John Dick unite together in order to lure the unhappy woman into the trap. At their instigation an English banker at Rome, Jenkins, presents himself before her, offering her unlimited credit on the part of Hamilton, and at the same time a Russian officer brings her, in the name of Alexis Orlof, the most flattering of imaginable declarations. *Le Balafré* declares himself convinced of the authenticity of the document whose existence she has made known to him, and highly disposed to avenge on Catherine the wrongs she has done his brother and himself. He asks the pretender to come and join him at Pisa. In vain does Domanski, whose sincere passion renders him clairvoyant, urge upon her not to go. She silences him : she will go where her destiny calls her.

At Pisa she is received as a sovereign. She has by this time again changed her name, and calls herself the Countess Silinska. Orlof showers upon her every manifestation of respect, in which there is a cunning tinge of sentiment. Watched always by the suspicious Domanski, he spares no pains to dazzle and to reassure his victim ; now giving way to wrathful exclamations against Catherine and her new favourite, now expressing an enthusiastic zeal in the cause of the pretender, and an almost servile subjection to her least desires, now suggesting a discreet passion which he scarcely dares avow, and with which he seems to unite certain personal ambitions of his own. He gives *fête* after *fête*, over which she is called upon to preside ; he induces her several times to come to Leghorn, where John Dick vies with him in gallantry and lavish hospitality. Without abandoning her attitude of haughty reserve, she lets herself go on the fatal descent. In order to overcome her last suspicions, he finally tells her openly that he

desires to share with her the empire which he proposes
to conquer for her ; she goes through a form of marriage
or of betrothal, which he wishes to celebrate by a grand
naval spectacle, a mock-fight of his squadron off Leghorn.   To witness it, she must go on board the admiral's
ship.   For the last time Domanski warns her ; she hears
him with disdain.   She sets foot on the ship ; salvos of
artillery and cries of " Long live the Empress ! " which
she supposes to be addressed to herself, greet her ; and
suddenly the veil is torn from her eyes : Orlof has
vanished, she sees herself surrounded by soldiers who
appear to be anything but disposed to do her homage ;
Domanski and Czarnomski, who accompany her, draw
their swords to protect her ; they are immediately dis-
armed.   She is seized and confined in a cabin, where,
a few moments after, a soldier casts at her feet, without
a word, the ring which she had given a few days before
to the man whom she imagined was her husband.   She
writes a few lines to him ; the soldier to whom she
confides the message returns with an orange wrapped
up in a piece of paper, on which, carrying out the play
to the end, *le Balafré* has pretended to hide his reply :
he declares he is a prisoner like herself, and unable to
do anything for her.   The ship hoists anchor, Orlof
remains behind at Leghorn, and it is the valiant Greigh,
worthy of more honourable commissions, who has to
conduct the captive to St. Petersburg.

He treats her with a consideration which shows that
he looked upon her as no ordinary adventuress.   The
cabin where she is confined is the captain's.   She is
allowed two of her servants.   At St. Petersburg, where

she arrives on May 12 (24), 1775, Field-marshal Prince Galitzin is instructed to examine her. He sends in his first report two weeks afterwards: the prisoner is represented as a person of the middle height, thin, of good carriage, with black hair and brown eyes, in which there is a slight cast, the nose long and hooked, the air of an Italian, speaking French and German, not knowing a word of Russian. The doctors who examine her declare she is far on in consumption. She says her name is Elizabeth, and she is twenty-three years old. She pretends that she knows neither her nationality, nor her birth-place, nor the name of her father and mother. She has been brought up at Kiel, in Holstein, in the home of a Frenchwoman named Peret or Peran, and baptized as a Greek. At the age of nine she left Kiel. A woman of the country, called Catherine, and three men, she knows not of what nationality, accompanied her. She went through Russia, passing through St. Petersburg on the way. They tell her that they are taking her to her parents at Moscow. She came presently to Persia, to Bagdad, where a rich merchant named Hamet received her into his house. A Persian prince called Hali, who was also living under the roof of this Hamet, took her on to Ispahan, surrounding her with the greatest care and respect, and declaring that she was the daughter of the Empress Elizabeth. She lived at Ispahan till 1769. She then travelled to Europe with her protector, who made her dress as a man in passing through Russia. She once more passed through St. Petersburg, but stayed there only one night. Prince Hali, recalled to his own country by urgent affairs, quitted her at London, leaving her a store of precious stones, and a quantity of ingot gold. Then she went to Paris as a Persian princess. She denies that it was her own idea to send Alexis Orlof the will of the Empress Elizabeth. She received this document at Ragusa, without her knowing where it came from, accompanied by a letter advising her to send it to the commandant of the Russian fleet. She did so, hoping to gain some light on the origin or intention of this communication. She had always heard of the birthright which this document attributed to her, but she never paid much attention to it. Orlof was the first to convince her.

To this report Galitzin adds a letter of the young woman addressed to Catherine. She asks for an interview in the tone of a person demanding a right, and able rather to give than to receive favours. She writes: "I can bring about matters of great advantage to your empire. My proceedings prove it. I only require to be in a position to disprove all the stories that have been set on foot against me." She signs it "Elizabeth." "What an arrant wretch!" cries Catherine, as she reads the letter. "The audacity of her note exceeds everything. I begin to believe that she is mad." Galitzin is instructed to obtain a more sincere and serious confession. Every one knows that she is an adventuress. The best thing to do is to get her into a confidential vein, and find out who set her to act this comedy. As the confidences do not arrive, the Empress sets about a personal investigation, with the result that she comes to the conviction that the unknown is the daughter of an innkeeper at Prague. It is from Gunning, the English envoy, that she declares she has the information. In his dispatches to the Foreign Office, Gunning does not seem so well informed. He is convinced, however, that she is an adventuress and an actress, and not too good an actress either. He treats the whole affair very lightly.

At a month's end, Galitzin sends in a second report, without having learnt anything further. When he speaks to her of the innkeeper of Prague, she declares that if she knew who had invented the fable she would tear his eyes out. She has never set foot in the city. Domanski, interrogated in turn, can give no further indication. He declares that he is prepared to spend the rest of his days in prison if he is permitted to marry the princess. When she is told of it, she replies that Domanski is a fool, who cannot even speak foreign languages, and whom she has never treated as anything but a servant. The field-marshal tries every scheme in vain, even depriving her of food and other necessities of life. There are men who never leave her day or night, ready to seize a moment of weakness in the part she is playing. Once more she asks leave to write to the Empress. The note, this time without signature, is couched in more humble language. She implores the Empress to pardon her if she has unwittingly offended her, to hear her, and to be her judge. She adds that " her condition makes nature shudder."

The only progress that is made is in the disease of the lungs from which she suffers. A priest is brought to her. But he endeavours to confess her on the subject of her life and adventures, and she immediately waves him aside: "Say the prayer for the dead: that is all that remains for you to do here."

She dies on December 4, 1775, in the fortress of St. Peter and Paul. A little before, Alexis Orlof had written to the Empress to say that he would be obliged to give up his position as commandant of the fleet, on account of the indignation roused against him in Italy by his abduction of the pseudo-Elizabeth. His life was no longer in safety in the country. Nevertheless a letter from Catherine, dated May 22, 1775, had expressed entire approval of his conduct. As we have several times had occasion to point out, the widow of Peter III. was naturally inclined to be indulgent towards adventurers, only they must be very careful not to come in the way of her own adventure, whose success was so important alike to herself and to Russia.

PART III.

PRIVATE LIFE.—COURT LIFE

CHAPTER I.

THE FAVOURITES.

I.

I SHALL not, I trust, be accused of seeking in this chapter any other kind of interest save the purely historic interest which has been my sole end in this study. I am not responsible for the existence of Gregory Orlof and his rivals in the history of Catherine, any more than I should be for that of Madame du Barry in the history of Louis XV. To draw a veil over her favourites would be, besides, to go directly against the wish of the great sovereign herself, for she never attempted to do it ; she wished them to be seen and admired. We shall not go to the point of admiration ; but to treat them as a matter of no consequence would be to go against historical truth : they are too conspicuous, they occupy too large a space ; to throw over them the veil which we cast over the too shameful shames of poor humanity would be still more offensive to Catherine, by lowering their part to a level too degrading alike for her and for them. In 1775, writing to the Empress, and alluding to the rumours which point out a certain successor to

Patiomkin, Sievers ventures to express very clearly his hopes in regard to the choice of the next favourite ; especially that he should have no influence in the Government. That is precisely what Catherine does not wish. She wishes that these men, her heart's choice or merely the companions of her pleasures, should have a large place, not only in her life, but in that of the country under her sway. And this is why some of them have already figured in this volume, for they really play a part in history. These are the most interesting. It will be found, I hope, that the others too have an interest of their own.

They are curiously unlike one another. From the first to the last there is a variety and a gradation of traits, or at least of *nuances*, very interesting to observe, for they show a corresponding modification in the tastes, instincts, and habits of Catherine, if not in her ways of thinking and feeling. Thus it is that their history is closely connected with that of the intellectual and moral development of the extraordinary woman whose companions they were. To neglect these details would be to lose a chance of studying the past psychologically, which perhaps is the most interesting way of studying it.

With the Orlofs, Patiomkin, and Zubofs, of whom we have already spoken in another chapter of this volume, we should also omit here the early companions, the Tshernishofs, Saltykof, and Poniatowski, whom we have introduced to our readers in a preceding volume, and who, as lovers of the Grand-Duchess, never had from the Empress the classic rank and title of "favourites."

These only come on the scene after the *coup d'État* of
1762, with Gregory Orlof. After him the list is long,
and we have no intention of exhausting it ; all we need
do is to give a brief indication of the principal names.

The first in date is purely and simply the first man
who comes along, the man to whom one beckons from a
window as he passes outside.

" A lieutenant of the horse-guards, named Vassiltshikof, who had chanced to be sent in the spring to
Tsarskoïe-Sielo, . . . has attracted the sovereign's attention, to every one's surprise, for he is not a distinguished-
looking person, he has never tried to push himself
forward, and is little known in society. The first sign
that Her Imperial Majesty gave him of her good graces
was when she left Tsarskoïe-Sielo to go to Peterhof :
she sent him a box of gold, saying that it was for having
kept such good order among the troops . . . It was
supposed to be a matter of no consequence. The
assiduities of this officer at Peterhof, his anxiety to be
always in the Empress's way, a sort of eagerness on her
part to distinguish him in the crowd, the much greater
ease and gaiety that she has had since her former
favourite's departure, the ill-humour and discontent of
the relations and friends of the latter ; in short, a
thousand other little details have at last opened the
courtiers' eyes."

It is thus that the Baron de Solms announces the
news to Frederick II., under date August 3, 1772. A
month after, he writes again :

" I have just seen M. Vassiltshikof, and I remembered
having met him often enough at the court, where he was

lost in the crowd.   He is a man of medium height, about twenty-eight years of age, very dark, and rather good-looking.   He has always been very polite to every-body, and has very amiable, but retiring manners, which he still retains.   It appears that he is rather embarrassed by the part he plays . . . Most people at the court dis-approve of the affair.   It causes some consternation to them, to the family and friends of Count Orlof, and to the ladies and gentlemen-in-waiting.   They all have an air of discontent and dejection.   They were all familiar with Count Orlof; he favoured and protected them.   Vas-siltshikof is unknown ; no one knows if he will have the same power as the other, and on whose behalf he will employ it.   The Empress is in the best of humours, always happy and contented, and given up entirely to *fêtes* and pleasures."

Catherine is now forty-three, and Gregory Orlof is in Moldavia, suspecting nothing.   The general disapproval of this new installation extends to the diplomatic body, and the English minister, Gunning, writes very severely in regard to this new caprice of the Tsarina, which seems to him a stain on a character so generally and so justly admired in other respects.   In addition to this, this little court revolution, prepared by Panin, instigated by Bariatinski, insignificant as it is in itself, has a political signification : it is the revenge of the aristocratic party, long displeased by the presence of the parvenu Orlof at the Empress's side.   The family of Vassiltshikof, the issue of the ancient boyards, and at one time allied with that of the Tolstois, is of illustrious origin ; in 1575 it gave a Tsarina to Russia.   It is but a short revenge :

the place that had been filled for ten years by the hand-some Gregory and his four brothers is too great a place for the new-comer to fill. He does but occupy it pass-ingly, before giving way to a more suitable successor. When Patiomkin appears, he disappears. *Saltavit et placuit.* His services are handsomely acknowledged, he marries, and marries happily.

In 1776, taking advantage of an imprudent absence of some weeks on the part of Patiomkin, Panin, this time acting in concert with Orlof, succeeds in securing the triumph of a new candidate, of very different type. Ukranian by origin, once prompter at the court theatre, then director of the secret department of Field-marshal Rumiantsof, governor of Little Russia, Zavadovski is a man of intelligence, accomplishment, and experience. This it is which renders him so formidable to the future conqueror of the Crimea, who is a whole year before he can get rid of him. At last he succeeds by making the discovery of Zoritch.

Zoritch is the only foreigner among all the imperial favourites; and he is of Sclavonic origin, Serbian or Croat. A Courlandais, Manteuffel, is supposed to have been invited to occupy the envied, if not enviable post, and to have declined the invitation. But Catherine seems to have generally had the will and wisdom to confine her caprices to Russians. The remembrance of Bühren probably served her in good stead in this. The son of a lieutenant-colonel in the Russian service, having himself served as lieutenant during the Seven Years' War, as major during the first Turkish war, Zoritch is already a man of mature years. However, in spite of

all the ordeals he has gone through, the several years'
captivity among the Turks, the bagnio at Constantinople, he is still, at the age of forty, a model of manly
beauty and vigour. Méhée de la Touche, who sees
him ten years later, when he is in retirement, thus
describes him :

" He is a man of five feet six, made to be painted.
I fancy he is near fifty, but his eyes are still charming,
and his manners full of grace. Though he is not lack-
ing in natural intelligence, his conversation is not infinitely piquant . . . He said to me over and over
again that he was once a barbarian, and that ' his lady '
had made another man of him. He spoke a good deal
to me of the days when he was in favour, and told me,
with tears in his eyes, of the kindnesses with which ' his
lady' had honoured him."

He is, indeed, a barbarian, but Catherine takes the
utmost pains in cultivating him, in order to lead the
way to a more intimate education still, in which her
scientific and literary tastes, and at the same time her
thwarted maternal instincts, find satisfaction. Zoritch
is neither young enough nor docile enough to lend himself easily to the experiment. And, unfortunately for
him, his pride marches ahead faster than his intelligence
or his knowledge. Named count in 1778, he affects
to scorn a title which he considers beneath him. He
desires to be a prince, like Orlof and Patiomkin.
Nothing more is needed to set the latter in search of
a new candidate for an office which creates such boundless ambitions. After some unfortunate attempts, in
which figure, first, a Persian, endowed with extraordi-

nary physical advantages (there are a large number
of exotics, as we know, in the suite of the luxurious
guardian of the seraglio whom Catherine has found for
herself), then the minister of police, Arharof, then
Zavadovski himself, the ex-favourite, taken up as a
last resource, and finally the man of the situation is
found : a common sergeant in the hussars, named
Korsak.

Zoritch does not take his dismissal without some
resistance. He talks of cutting off the ears of any
hussar who tries to dislodge him from his place. He
even challenges his former protector to a duel ; but
Patiomkin refuses to fight with him, and Catherine
herself interferes and promptly settles the Serbian's
dismissal. His favour has lasted eleven months (1777—
78). He retires, finally, with about four hundred thousand livres of income, and the estate of Shklof in White
Russia, the revenue of which is double that amount.
It is still Poland that pays for his pension. After
living abroad for some months, he retires finally to
his estate, which is a sort of principality. He lives
there almost like a king, with a large court, a theatre
where he mounts French operas and Italian ballets at
immense cost. He founds there the famous military
school, where two hundred youths are brought up at
his expense, but which is often on the verge of ruin,
the funds destined to its maintenance having been
squandered by the boundless extravagance of the
former favourite. In one night he loses fifty thousand
roubles, which are won by a Prince Volkonski.

In 1780, on her way to meet Joseph II. at Mohilef,

Catherine stops at Shklof. Zoritch entirely re-builds the superb castle in which he lives, and places in the new building an exact copy of the bedroom in the Winter Palace, which he remembers in every detail. We are not aware whether he does the honours of the situation to his august visitor in exact accordance with the *mise-en-scène*. But he expends sixty thousand roubles on Saxe porcelain, on which Frederick makes him pay double dues of entrance and export in passing through his states, in order to punish him for not having bought it at Berlin.

In 1783 the lord of Shklof, whose affairs are getting more and more complicated, is suspected of taking part in a fabrication of false money-orders, which are discovered near his house. He clears himself of the charge, and even re-appears at the court after Catherine's death, and holds a place there till the time of his death, in 1799.

In the series at which we have briefly glanced, Zoritch was the fine male *par excellence ;* Korsak is the tenor. Writing to Grimm, May 7, 1779, Catherine assures the " fag " that he could not choose but weep if he heard him sing, as he did when hearing Gabrielli, the famous *prima donna*, daughter of a cook of Prince Gabrielli, whose name she chose to take with her from capital to capital, St. Petersburg included, where her *roulades* have left never-to-be-forgotten memories, as also her *liaison* with a high official of the court, the senator Ielaguine, the same who had the doubtful privilege of entertaining Cagliostro. This time he sprains his ankle in trying to do *pirouettes* before the fair singer. The

reign of the new favourite opens a new epoch in the
annals of musical art in Russia.   As partners for him
the most famous Italian artistes are welcomed on the
shores of the Neva: the illustrious Corilla Olimpica,
the friend of Alexis Orlof, comes to mingle the inspired
accents of her poetic improvisations with the melodious
voice of the handsome singer; the violinist Nadini, so
highly appreciated in France, where he dies in 1799,
is permitted the honour of accompanying him; and
Catherine writes to her confidant: "Do you know that
we go in for art, science, music, etc., more than ever . . .
I have never seen any one who more really delighted
in all the sounds of harmony than Pyrrhus, king of
Epirus."

"Pyrrhus, king of Epirus," is Korsak, or Korsakof,
as he is now called.   Catherine has always had a taste
for nicknames, though for the most part it is now
impossible to see the point of them.   There is no apparent likeness between Zoritch's successor and the
famous conqueror of Macedonia.   Korsak seems to
have been his real name, and it is that of a very old
Polish family, still very honourably represented, but
never having pretended to a specially illustrious origin.
After the rise of the favourite, this name, Russified by
the termination *of*, apparently to soothe the suscepti-
bilities of national *amour propre*, is associated with a
genealogy made up of all kinds of scraps, and beginning
with these words: "To go no further back, we begin
with Hercules."   There had indeed been Korsakofs in
Russia, but these were connections neither of the lover
of Omphale nor of the lover of Catherine.   One at least

is known to history, the vice-governor of a certain province in 1715, condemned to the knout for private misdeeds. He was no relation of the favourite.

Created general aide-de-camp, knight of the Polish Eagle, and chamberlain, and overwhelmed with the customary honours and presents, Korsak or Korsakof applied himself to justify these liberalities : he was already artistic in his tastes, he would be a man of science as well. He orders a bookseller to supply him with a library.

"What books would your lordship like to possess ?"

"You know what I want! Big volumes below and small volumes above, like the Empress's."

Evidently those afternoons passed in *tête-à-tête* with the Empress in the midst of the precious collections of the Hermitage were not thrown away. Unfortunately he was delicate in health, subject to blood-spitting ; his heart too was constitutionally weak, and the Empress one day surprises him in the arms of the Countess Bruce, who also makes a point of loving artists. A door which happens to open at the wrong moment reveals this community of sentiments to Catherine ; and Patiomkin is supposed to have had his part in the accident. Perhaps he found it a good occasion to pay off a grudge against his eternal enemy, Field-marshal Rumiantsof, of whom the Countess Bruce was the sister. Perhaps he merely thought that the favourite had lasted long enough. He had lasted fifteen months, and had cost Catherine about a million of roubles : tenors as a rule do not cost so much as that, even now-a-days. Countess Bruce was banished for a time to Moscow, where the disgraced favourite followed her, and where he quietly lived to an advanced age. Catherine was always considerate for her weaknesses in the past, no doubt feeling that it was one way of assuring that others would be so for her weaknesses in the future.

II.

"I did not expect to hear my letter to the historian described as a masterpiece. It is true that General Lanskoï told me that it was charming, but any young man, whatever tact he may have, easily becomes enthusiastic, and especially a warm soul like his. Now, to know what this man is like, I must tell you the phrase of Prince Orlof on the subject to one of his friends : 'Oh,' said he, 'you will see what he will turn out. He gobbles up everything.' He began by gobbling up the poets and poems one winter, several historians the next. Novels bore me, and we trifle with Algarotti and his like. Without having studied, we have numberless acquirements, and we live with delight in the company of all that is best and most learned. Besides that, we build and we plant, we are benevolent, gay, honest, and as amiable as can be."

These lines, in which Catherine's style is plainly recognizable, the style of her epistolary conversations with Grimm, are dated June 1782, and, in alluding to a letter recently sent by her to Buffon, the sovereign points out the progress of the new scholar whom she has taken in hand. He arouses her warmest hopes. In the book

which takes up, awkwardly enough, the defence of Catherine and her court against the "disgusting work of
Masson," Kotzebue is unjust to this young man: " M.
Lanskoï was the most ignorant man of the court of
Catherine, the Empress herself blushed when he spoke
to her." This must be taken with due allowance. At
the moment when Catherine set eyes on him, the
favourite was doubtless, at the age of twenty-two,
neither more nor less ignorant than the majority of his
comrades in the Guards. But the Tshernishofs and the
Orlofs had already taught Catherine twenty years before
not to be too particular on this subject, and her court
never was or professed to be an information bureau.
Belonging to the lesser nobility, Lanskoï doubtless had
the same education as the greater part of the courtiers :
he could read and write in Russian, and say a few words
in French. When Catherine took it into her head, in
1784, to make him correspond with her literary friends
in the West, she had to act as his secretary. The letters
of the favourite to Grimm, dated this year, are, from
first word to last, in the hand of the Empress. Here
are some specimens :

" You see, Monsieur " (Lanskoï is supposed to be
dictating to Catherine), " what sort of a secretary I
have ; he says that mine was as stupid as an owl ; for my
part, I really believe that it is jealousy which makes
people talk like that. I should be very pleased with
this one if he would only write my ideas instead of
his."

In the following letter the favourite announces to the
" fag " that he is sending him 50,000 roubles for the

purchase of the collection of pictures to be sold by the Comte de Baudoin, and he adds:

"If you require more than that, the rest will be sent as soon as the news reaches your most humble servant or his secretary, with whose name, Monsieur, you are not acquainted, nor with his writing, he informs me. This secretary is, as you know, a very good and clever personage, whom I am glad to praise in passing, all the more so as he does his duty admirably; he is diligent, quick, gay, and altogether a jolly fellow; he gives me the use of his pen without charge, and sometimes more than I want of his advice. He tells me that you find him quite a character."

A single letter, dated May 31, 1784, is in Lanskoï's writing; it is very correctly expressed, but short and insignificant: a scholar's task, done as well as he knows how to do it. "He did his best, he was learning," wrote Catherine after his death. He took lessons in French from a Chevalier de Serres with whom he had been friendly before his elevation. The latter was fond of telling that the fortune of Lanskoï, just before he became the most opulent lord in Russia, consisted in five shirts. One night, finding himself without a roof over his head, Lanskoï came and knocked at the door of his friend. De Serres considered that he was doing all he need do in letting him sleep by the side of his bed, on the floor of his modest room. A few weeks later, then in residence in the favourite's apartments at the Winter Palace, Lanskoï sent for his former host, treated him in the most friendly way, gave him supper, begged him to stay over night, went to bed, and

requested him to do the same—on the floor.   De Serres
had to do it, not without bad dreams, assuredly.

Not content with learning French, the favourite also
endeavoured to acquire a taste for the beautiful things
with which he saw that Catherine loved to surround
herself.   "He nearly fainted," if we may believe
Catherine, on learning that Grimm had let slip, without
buying them for him, a precious collection of antique
gems.   So far as we can judge, he was an insignificant
and agreeable young man.   Discovered and brought
forward by Patiomkin, he had, in the eyes of the latter,
the advantage of not showing signs of any pretentions
beyond those naturally belonging to his office.   Naturally
indolent, he even discouraged Catherine's ambitions on
his behalf.   Any kind of participation in the affairs of
state was averse to him, perhaps on account of his good
sense as well as his idleness.   His mistress was obliged
to content herself with giving him the outer pomp of
merely decorative dignities.   She made him, as she had
made the others, general, chamberlain, head of her
regiment of cuirassiers, grand cross of the Polar Star!
She wrote to Chrapowiçki to know if the famous Golden
Book of the Russian nobility, the *Barhatnaïa Kniga*
(Velvet Book), had nothing about his ancestors; and in
money, palaces, lands, and diamonds, she gave him the
enormous sum of seven millions of roubles (about thirty-
five million francs).   In this respect, there was no
refusal on his part: he loved money.   He also loved
drink: the memoirs of his time have preserved the
receipt of a punch of his invention, a mixture of Tokay,
rum, and the juice of pine-apple, which he frequently

drank to excess. He also had a troublesome family, terrible brothers, who often crop up in the correspondence of Catherine at the time with Grimm. The sovereign sends them travelling abroad, and sees that they do not get into too much trouble ; the favourite himself paying very little heed to the matter, careless in this respect also, nowise inclined to nepotism. The burden fell principally on the shoulders of the imperial " fag," who was sometimes almost overwhelmed by it. In 1782 he put in motion the French authorities at Bar-le-Duc to arrest one of these troublesome brothers, and put him in prison, in order to separate him from a woman who had captivated him. The archives of the Minister of Foreign Affairs show some traces of this romance.

In 1784 the favour of Lanskoï has lasted four years, and, contrary to all anticipation, it seems in no likelihood of lessening : Patiomkin is always satisfied with him, and Catherine idolizes him. But a fell malady assails his strength : a scarlet fever, complicated with angina, both aggravated by the premature exhaustion of an organism artificially excited and sustained for some length of time. The memoirs of the German physician, Weickhardt, one of those who tended him, contain brutally instructive indications in this respect. Perhaps indeed the doctor revenged himself on the insults which he had to undergo at the hands of the patient. Lanskoï joked at his hump, declared that he could not suffer the sight of his enormous nose, and made fun of his medicines. Sitting on her lover's bed, Catherine amused herself with his petulance. In medical science she was rather the pupil of Molière than of Voltaire, and she refused to admit the possibility of serious danger for one whose health she had reason to believe was so vigorous. "You do not know what a strong constitution he has," she told Weickhardt. The German shook his head, saying to himself that cantharides powder may well pass for strength of constitution, but it is a destructive strength. While refusing the attendance of Weickhardt, Lanskoï accepted that of his ordinary doctor, the Russian Sobolevski, and that of his *valet de chambre*, generally drunk, who would bring him wine on the sly. His throat was on fire, he would not allow any one to touch it. But when the disease took a deeper hold of him, he immediately called in a surgeon, and submitted to the application of *blanc de céruse :* this time, he declared, his future was at stake. So, at least, Weickhardt relates.

A choking fit carried him off on June 25, 1784. We have elsewhere spoken of the sorrow of Catherine. Alexander Vorontsof, who certainly cannot be suspected of a prejudice on behalf of the sovereign, and who is generally ready enough to look upon her amorous exaltations as being merely a comedy of sentiment, goes so far, this time, as to believe that she will not survive her loss. "Affairs have been entirely suspended since the death of M. Lanskoï," writes the French *chargé d'affaires*, Caillard, under date July 13, "and no one thinks of anything but of the Empress herself, whose state of health is somewhat alarming." Two months later, the sovereign only sees her ministers at rare intervals, and then only to ask them, "sadly and tenderly," if all is well, after which she dismisses them, and shuts herself up in her room with Madame Kushelof, a sister of the deceased favourite. This person was not supposed to have a very warm affection for her brother, but she has the gift of tears. Whenever she sees the Empress she bursts into tears; the Empress does likewise, and they pass their time in this dismal *tête-à-tête.* In her correspondence with Grimm, which is not interrupted even now, Catherine denies that she has neglected her duty: "As for public affairs," she writes, "they go on as usual; but as for myself, who had enjoyed so great a private happiness, I have nothing left to enjoy. I bury myself in tears and in writing, and that is all... If you would know exactly my state, I will tell you that since three months yesterday I have been inconsolable for the irreparable loss that I have suffered; that the only improvement in things is, that I am accustomed again to seeing human faces; that, in spite of all, my heart bleeds as at the first moment; that I do my duty, and endeavour to do it well, but that my sorrow is extreme, and such as I have never had in my life; and it is now three months that I have been in this cruel situation, suffering the tortures of the damned."

Let us not forget that she is now fifty-five, and thus thirty years older than when, at the time of a merely momentary separation, she wrote to Zahar Tshernishof:

"The first day it was as if I were waiting for you, so accustomed am I to see you; the second, I was moody, and avoided company; the third, I was desperately *ennuyée;* the fourth, appetite and sleep abandoned me, all things became insupportable to me ; no more toilets, etc. ; the fifth, I gave myself up to tears . . . Must I still further call things by their true name ? Well then, I love you ! "

And on the eve of the day of his return : " What a day for me will to-morrow be ! Shall I find it all that I dream ? No, never will any one love you as I love you. Restless, I take up a book; I try to read ; at every line, you interrupt me ; I throw the book aside, I throw myself on the sofa, I try to sleep, but how ? For two hours that I have been lying there I have not closed my eyes ; and I am only a little calmer since I have begun to write to you. I have a good mind to bare my arm to be bled again ; perhaps that will distract me."

At last, towards the middle of October, Patiomkin, who is still absent, and to whom she has sent courier after courier to hasten his return, arrives at Tsarskoïe, where the Empress still prolongs her stay, in spite of the severity of the autumn ; he induces her to return to St. Petersburg. Her return, however, manifests a change in her habits, and a mental trouble, equally extra-ordinary in her. Without giving warning to any one, she sets out for the Winter Palace, where she finds the gates closed and no one to receive her ; goes on to the Hermitage, where all is equally closed and deserted ; has the gates forced open, goes to bed, then, waking at one o'clock in the morning, orders the salvos of artillery which usually announce her return to be fired, puts the whole city in consternation by this nocturnal cannonade, calls out the garrison and drives

her attendants to distraction, and seems surprised herself
to have caused such an upset. But, a few days afterwards, she gives audience to the diplomatic body, and
appears as composed in body and mind, as affable and
smiling, as usual.

And ere long her life returns to its usual course, and
the eternal lover returns to life. On the mausoleum
which is erected in the cemetery of Tsarskoïe, an inscription, carelessly inscribed, does not even give the right
date of the day on which occurred the death of the man
so deeply loved and lamented. A few months afterwards the inconsolable lover begins to reason, in her
conversation with Grimm, in almost an impersonal
manner, concerning her grief: " I have always said that
this magnetism which cures no one, at all events kills no
one either." A month later, and the grief is dead: " I
have become calm and serene once more," she writes,
"because, with the help of my friends, I have made an
effort over myself. We began with a comedy, which
every one says was charming; this then proves the
return of vigour and gaiety. The monosyllables are
banished, and " (now comes the real reason of this return
to the ways and distractions of the past) " I can no
longer complain of not having those about me whose
cares and affection are calculated to cheer and distract
me, but it needed some time to accustom oneself to it."

It needed some time! Ten months, to a day, to the
date of this letter, which ends with this avowal: " In
short, in one word as in a hundred, I have a very capable
friend, and one well worthy of being so."

That he is very capable, we can easily believe. He is

called Jermolof, and he is an agreeable companion. The following summer is one of the gayest and most lively that Catherine has ever spent. However, in the moving constellation where Lanskoï has just been eclipsed, and Mamonof is about to appear, this new love is only a star of the second magnitude. Naturally, after the sorrowful crisis that she has just passed through, Catherine is not prepared to let herself go in one of those overwhelming attachments which, in this woman of sensual nature, are far from being mere impulses of the flesh, but are quite as much concerns. of heart and mind. This time there is neither passion nor even infatuation for the man whom she has taken up, almost without enthusiasm, coldly and tranquilly, as if she were making a reasonable marriage. Her choice is not, however, such a bad one. The man is better than his office. Bezborodko speaks of him as a modest, refined young man, who cultivates the society of serious people. He fears even that his timid manners, his reserve and love of decorum, may prove an obstacle to the continuance of his favour with a mistress whom Korsakof and Lanskoï have accustomed to quite other and much more piquant manners.

Nor is he mistaken, for in less than a year Catherine already seems to show signs of lassitude. The grandmaster of the imperial pleasures is not, it is true, a stranger to this prompt disenchantment: the favourite has shown to the Empress, before sending it on to his all-powerful protector, a letter from the ex-khan of the Crimea, Shahin-Guiraï, in retirement at Kalonga with a pension of two hundred thousand roubles, complaining of the exactions that Patiomkin levies upon his former subjects. Nothing more is needed ; in April 1786, Shahin-Guiraï and Jermolof both lose, the one his pension, the other his place as favourite.

The new crisis, which is oddly like those which modern parliamentary methods bring about periodically in the organization of governments, lasts several months, during which Patiomkin's enemies do their utmost to bring in a candidate of their own. For a moment they seem to have won the day with Mengden of Courland, who seems on the point of being selected. But at last Patiomkin distances them with the young and fascinating Dmitrief Mamonof; and the event is one of considerable importance, a really national question. The Comte de Ségur rejoices in it greatly. " M. Jermolof," he writes, " honoured our nation, and myself in particular, with the most decided aversion, permitting himself the most unseemly remarks whenever France was alluded to, showing marked impertinence to me, and losing no occasion of stirring up the Empress's old prejudices against us. Though he had too little ability to gain serious credit, he was hand and glove with a party which has much, and which commenced to be a grave impediment to me."

III.

His successor, on the other hand, is entirely on the side of France. This time Patiomkin has put his hand on an accomplished man of the court, of education and

refined tastes. He even fears that the dish may be too
delicate for the palate to which it is destined. "The
design is good, but the colouring is not worth much,"
said Catherine, when she saw the portrait of the candidate. She lets herself be influenced, however, and soon
falls under the charm of the elegant courtier, the brilliant
talker, who perhaps calls up other recollections in her.
"I love, and all my life I shall love, Prince Poniatowski,"
she once wrote to Zahar Tshernishof. Of ancient
lineage, said even to be connected with Rurik, inscribed, certainly, in the "Velvet Book," the new-comer
flatters the new aristocratic tendencies of the sovereign.
Well versed in French literature, speaking several
languages fluently, writing plays, which, it is true, are
detestable, he naturally takes up the tone which the
Comte de Ségur has lately introduced into the Empress's
private circle. Joseph II., who makes his acquaintance
during the Crimean journey, refuses to see that he is
in place in these surroundings. "The new favourite,"
he writes to Field-marshal de Lascy, "is a young man
of twenty-six, without education, a mere child . . . a
nice-looking fellow enough, but seeming quite out of
his element, and without any particular intelligence."
This is perhaps, on the part of the Emperor, a touch of
jealousy or spite, provoked by the strange liberties that
Catherine tolerates and encourages in this "nice-looking
fellow," who does in fact give way sometimes to the
caprices of a spoilt child. It is unpleasant, when one is
an emperor, to be interrupted in the course of a game
of whist, in order that a mere gentleman of the court
may finish a caricature that he is drawing on the card-

table with the stick of white chalk which is still used in
Russia to mark the points. Ségur, the Prince de Ligne,
and their colleagues of the diplomatic world are less
particular : "full of wit, talk, and finesse," writes the
Saxon Sacken, in speaking of the favourite. And, in
spite of the caricatures, drawn at the wrong moment,
Joseph himself does not disdain to pay court, to some
extent, to this unskilful partner, presenting him with a
costly watch, and offering to make him Count of the
Holy Empire.

As for Catherine, she has the best reasons in the
world for not despising the wit and knowledge of her
new companion, for, unlike Lanskoï, it is now Mamonof
who holds the pen when she writes letters to Grimm.
He is sometimes a stubborn and unwilling secretary, for
we read in one of the letters thus written : "I dictated
something quite different, but *Red Coat* would not write
it. You will know in time what this Red Coat is, if you
do not know already."

Grimm could not fail to be sufficiently edified on this
subject ; but in order that he may be suitably so, she
writes :

"This Red Coat envelops a being who unites a great
fund of uprightness to a most excellent heart. As for
wit, he has enough for four, an unlimited fund of gaiety,
great originality in the conception of things and in the
way of rendering them, an admirable education, singularly instructed in all that can give brilliance to wit.
We hide our love for poetry as if it were murder ; we
are passionately fond of music ; our conception in all
things is of a rare facility. God only knows what we

know by heart. We declaim, we jest, we have the tone
of the best society ; we are excessively polite ; we write
in Russian and in French as few among us can write,
alike as regards the style and the temper. Our outer
responds perfectly to our inner man ; our features are
very regular ; we have two superb black eyes, with eyebrows outlined as one rarely sees ; above the middle
height, noble in manner, easy in demeanour ; in a word,
we are as solid within as we are agile, strong, and
brilliant without. I am convinced that if you met this
Red Coat, you would ask what his name was, if you did
not guess it at once."

The "fund of uprightness" that Catherine discovers
in a young man of twenty-six who sees no objection to
a mistress thirty years older than himself, bears witness
to an extreme power of self-deception. But it must be
said that she has met an actor of her own calibre, who
plays his part to the uttermost. On the occasion of the
meeting between the old Empress and the old Poniatowski on the Dnieper, in sight of Kaniof, the favourite
does not fail to give every evidence of a jealousy proper
to a man passionately in love. Ségur and the Prince
de Ligne hold their sides, but Catherine ingenuously
pities her lover's distress; at the conclusion of the interview, which, as we know, is passed in the exchange of
commonplace compliments, she feels obliged, in order
to ease his mind, to exaggerate the boredom she has
felt. And the letters that she writes shortly after to
Patiomkin show the intense delight which this little
scene has caused her : "Sasha is a priceless creature"
(Sasha being Mamonof). And Patiomkin himself is

worth his weight in gold for having given Sasha to
Catherine. Ingenuous as ever, she does not hesitate to
express her gratitude to him.

The favourite, however, is neither a *naïf* nor an un-
conscious person, nor even a cynic. " Some of them "
(the favourites), notes Langeron in his memoirs, " knew
how to ennoble this degrading office ; Patiomkin by
making himself almost emperor, Zavadovski by his
value in the administration of affairs, Mamonof by the
shame that he felt and did not attempt to conceal."
The latter part of the observation is carried out by
other testimonies. It seems to indicate a nature in
which the lower instincts have not altogether got the
mastery over a moral sensibility of higher order. Only
the price of the shame is too tempting, and the course
of action once decided upon, the young man shows
himself not less eager to defend and to make the most
of his possession. Garnovski, in his memoirs, shows
him to us discussing with Count Bruce in regard to an
estate which the latter wishes to sell, and which the
favourite longs and yet hardly dares to ask the Empress
to buy for him : he has just bought another for three
hundred and fifty thousand roubles. Bruce intimating
that he will have no difficulty in finding another purchaser, and the Empress, who is present at the interview,
pretending to take no notice of the mute invocations
that Mamonof addresses to her, Mamonof gives a sigh
of resignation :

" So be it. Who is this other purchaser ? "

" Kazarinof."

At that the favourite turns deathly pale ; he looks as

if about to faint. He stammers out, with a terrified glance at the Empress:

"But Kazarinof has nothing! How can he get such an amount of money?"

Catherine at last puts in her word. She has been on bad terms for the last few days with her lover, who has no doubt been somewhat negligent in the accomplishment of his duty, and she has given some encouragement to this Kazarinof, a young officer, who has long been endeavouring to attract her attention.

"Is there no one but Kazarinof in the world?" she says slowly, fixing her eyes on the favourite. "The purchaser will not perhaps be the one you think."

At that Mamonof does actually faint away. He is put in bed in a state of fever. The two court physicians, Rogerson and Messing, are greatly concerned. Only Ribeaupierre, whose hands the patient kisses in sign of gratitude, finds an infallible specific for his cure by bringing to his bedside the repentant Empress, happy to find herself so passionately loved.

The favourite sometimes takes his revenge by violent scenes in the manner of Patiomkin, generally on account of the part that he wishes to play in affairs. Catherine herself wishes it to be considerable : one day she scolds her secretary, Chrapowiçki, for having sent an important military document to the Field-marshal Saltykof, without first showing it to the favourite. But Mamonof is ambitious, even to the point of being jealous of Bezborodko, whose talents Catherine still appreciates. "I spit on his talents, on him, and all his gang!" he cries one day. She cries over it for a whole night, and then gives way to the demands of the favourite by putting a slight upon the minister.

At last there comes a day when this man, who has made of love a degrading instrument of his ambition and his fortune, sacrifices both the one and the other, in the cause of love. It is a regular drama which is acted out at the Hermitage and the Winter Palace, a drama which was indeed put on the stage by Madame Birch-Pfeiffer in *The Favourites*, acted at Berlin in 1831. After the first performance, which had been calmly witnessed by the German princesses, great-grandchildren of Catherine, the Russian envoy, Count Ribeaupierre, son of the obliging physician who had cured the imperial favourite, forbids the continuance of the piece, to the great disgust of Mesdames Kreslinger and Hagen, who had created the parts of the Empress and her rival, " in such a manner," says Ribeaupierre in his memoirs, " that they deserved to be driven off the stage."

On the 20th of June, 1789, as she is working with Chrapowiçki, Catherine suddenly interrupts the reading of a report :

" Have you heard what has happened ? "

" Yes, Madame."

" I have been suspecting it now for eight months. He withdrew from everybody. He even avoided me. It was always an oppression of the chest which obliged him to remain in his room. Then, lately, he began to speak of scruples of conscience which distressed him, and would not allow him to continue living with me. The traitor ! It was this other love, it was his duplicity, which weighed upon him ! But if he could not overcome it, why did he not tell me frankly? He has been in love with her for a year! If he had spoken, what happened three days ago would have happened half a year sooner, and he cannot imagine what I have suffered!"

"Every one is surprised that Your Majesty has given consent to the marriage."

"God be with them: I hope they will be happy. . . . But, look you, I have pardoned them, I have authorized their union, they ought to be in ecstasies: well, they are both of them wretched. Ah, the old affection is not dead in him yet. For a week and more he follows me with his eyes constantly. Strange! . . . Once, do you remember, he cared for so many things, everything was so easy to him; now he gets confused in whatever he does, everything bores him, his chest is always unwell! The prince said to me this winter: '*Matushka*, spit on her!' And he pointed to the Shtcherbatof. But I was blind, and I tried to excuse him!"

This is not a dialogue of Madame Birch-Pfeiffer that I give; it is a page from the journal of the exact and conscientious Chrapowiçki, word for word.

Mademoiselle Shtcherbatof was a maid-of-honour, and as such she lived in the imperial palace, without being able to absent herself without a special authorization, and then only to visit her nearest relatives. This circumstance aided Mamonof and her in the *liaison* whose *dénouement* we have just learnt. And Catherine, talking with her secretary, tells us further how she came to discover this singular infidelity.

"On Monday, the 18th of June, he came to me, and

complained of my coldness. I told him that he knew well what it was, since September last, and how much I had suffered. You pay no attention to what I say, now for a long time, I said to him ; but since a separation has become necessary, I will look after your future. Thereupon I sent him a note which assured to him, on retiring, a brilliant position, and at the same time the idea occurred to me of a marriage for him with the daughter of Count Bruce. She is only thirteen, but she is already mature : I know that. At that he comes to me, trembling, and confesses that he is in love with the Shtcherbatof, and had promised her marriage half a year ago. Imagine what I felt! "

The pathetic monologue of the old lover abandoned by love continues longer yet, but, while she pours out her complaints and sad reflections, Catherine also gives orders : first a costly ring, then bank-notes for ten thousand roubles, are brought to her. She hands the ring and the money to Chrapowicki, who knows what he is to do with them. The conversation takes place, as usual, in the Empress's bedroom. The secretary rises discreetly, and places what has been handed to him under the pillow of the great bed, which that very evening is to become a nuptial bed : the ring and the ten thousand roubles are for the young and fascinating Zubof, whom Anna Naryshkin, the devoted friend, has introduced into the palace at the very outset of the crisis.

Mamonof's marriage takes place eight days later. According to custom, the bride's toilet takes place in the Empress's rooms, with her own assistance. An eye-witness relates that as the Empress touches her head-

dress the girl gives a cry of pain : a gold hair-pin has
run into her head.   Other rumours speak of a horrible
attack on the young couple a few days after : masked
men rush into the room, tear the wife from the arms of
her husband, and flog her before his very eyes.   All
that we know of Catherine's treatment of her former
lover strongly contradicts these stories.   On leaving St.
Petersburg, Mamonof receives a present of three thousand peasants and a sum of a hundred thousand roubles,
which is paid down in spite of the penury in which the
imperial treasury is at the moment.   He even pretends,
to those about him, that, like Patiomkin, he preserves,
even in retirement, the privileges of the office which he
has left, and the influence connected with it.   No doubt
Catherine is deeply wounded, to the extent even of
injustice towards her best friend, whose warnings she
has however neglected.   She does not remember them
now, and she writes to the conqueror of the Crimea :
" You would have cured me in an instant if you had
told me the truth . . . I have never been the tyrant of
any one, and I hate constraint. . . . Is it possible that
you did not know me on this point . . . and that you
imagined me a miserable egoist ? "   But there is more
of sorrow than of anger in her reproaches.   As for
Patiomkin, he arranges things his own way : Mamonof
is a fool ; how could he so stupidly leave a place which
he had been meant to keep ?   But it is no great loss.
He does not remember that he himself was the first
protector of the favourite and the promoter of his
fortune.   He writes : " In my way of looking at things,
I have never been mistaken in him : he is a mixture of

indolence and egoism. In the latter he was Narcissus to excess. Never thinking of any one but himself, he expected everything without giving anything in return. Lazy as he was, he forgot even what was seemly. No matter whether or not a thing has any value, the moment it pleases him, it becomes the most valuable thing in the world. That is how he looks on Princess Shtcherbatof!"

Catherine comes finally to find consolation in the idea, which is suggested to her by the ever-serviceable Ribeaupierre, that the former favourite has gone mad, like Orlof: "Can you conceive that he actually wanted to remain with his wife at the court, as before? What a contradictory notion!" And she has neither leisure nor inclination to indulge in a very lengthy resentment, for her letters, in the following month, are already full of another matter for concern: to gain the good graces of her distant friend, busy waging war against the Turks, for "an innocent soul," who has been enchanted to find a nice ring and a big packet of bank-notes under a luxurious pillow, and who has a thirst for caresses: "Come, my friend, send *us* some caresses so that we may be quite happy." She is once more full of her old gaiety, which only Lanskoï (already so soon forgotten!) had been able to check for a time; and it is in the easiest way in the world that she explains the awkward incident to Grimm a little later on. "The pupil of Mademoiselle Cardel having found the Red Coat worthy rather of pity than of anger, and punished for life by this silliest of passions, which has not put the laughers on his side, and has only won him the repute of ingratitude, she has merely put an end to all that, to the satisfaction of the interested parties, at the earliest opportunity . . . There is reason to believe that the domestic arrangements do not get on well at all."

Did the marriage really turn out so badly? The correspondence of Catherine with the ex-favourite, beginning immediately after their separation and going on to 1795, has been published. Quite commonplace, at first, on both sides, these letters change their tone after a few years, and indicate, in Mamonof at least, a state of mind little encouraging with regard to the domestic virtues. In December 1792, the ex-favourite makes a confession : he is profoundly miserable. Doubtless the sovereign's bounties have afforded him an enviable situation in many respects, but the regret of no longer seeing her leaves him no room for any other feeling of pleasure. Banished to Moscow since his marriage, he has but one desire: to return to St. Petersburg and to her from whom, for his happiness' sake, he should never have separated. And so strong is the illusion in the mind of the amorous woman of sixty, insatiable of love as at twenty, that she has not even a moment's surprise on reading these amazing confessions. " I am sure of it," she calmly says to Chrapowiçki, " he cannot be happy." And she almost begins to consider the consequences of a return to the past. But no, Zubof is there, and " it is another thing to go into the garden with him and see him for four hours, another thing to live with him." And if he returned, the old life together would no doubt begin over again. She fears this eventuality, and, in a tender and touching letter, she puts off for a year the meeting desired by the audacious sycophant, to whom Patiomkin, who is endeavouring to fight the new favourite, has probably suggested it. But in the following year it is Mamonof in turn, who, invited to pay the visit he had so ardently desired, recoils before the now established position of Zubof, and before the terrible prospect of measuring arms (Patiomkin being now no more) with so powerful a rival. Zubof is to have no successor.

CHAPTER II.

THE CORRESPONDENTS.—GRIMM.

I.

BUSINESS letters, properly speaking, orders or instructions addressed to subordinates, exchange of compliments or of diplomatic confidences with other sovereigns, make up a comparatively small amount of Catherine's correspondence. She writes and receives a great number of letters, and those she writes, like those she receives, are often very long ; but this epistolary abundance and prolixity are due mainly to two causes, both equally distinct from the ordinary necessities of government, if not entirely alien to them : in the first place an impulse to lavish herself and her ardent and exuberant nature, always requiring to express and communicate everything that she thinks and feels, or at least everything that she wishes people to think of her thoughts and feelings. In a word, she is loquacious. In the second place, she sees, in this extraordinarily extensive correspondence, into which she flings herself with such exceptional prodigality, a very powerful means of action. The letters that she receives

are, for the most part, a sort of political reporting,
adroitly set on foot and carried out ; those that she sends
are frequently a sort of official journalism.   They contain plans of campaign, explanatory statements, militant
articles, and even actual manifestoes, as in the letter of
January 21, 1791, addressed to Zimmermann, but intended for the court of Berlin, which she desires to
reassure, while advising it not to mix in the affairs of
Turkey.   A part of the letters to Voltaire are really
meant to shake the situation of the Duc de Choiseul ;
as she one day confesses to Chrapowiçki.

From this twofold point of view, her letters may be
divided into three categories : those that she writes,
those that she composes, and those that are composed
for her.   The first are the rarest, considerable as they
are : they are addressed to the one confidant, Grimm
and a few intimate friends, to the favourites during their
term of office, and to two or three of them after.   Short
notes hastily scribbled, or long chats, pen in hand, she
abandons herself to them, putting into them all that
enters her head, with the most perfect freedom, and at
the bidding of the most casual inspiration.   But she
writes twice over a note of a few lines in which she
informs the Prince de Ligne of her intention of making
a journey through the Crimea : here we see the work
of composition.   And there is probably not a single
one of her letters to Voltaire which, in form at any rate,
is entirely her own handiwork : it is literature made to
order.   It is only just to say that she has no pretensions in regard to it, though she does indeed sometimes
try to set people on the wrong scent as to her ways

of work. "I only write letters myself," she tells the Prince de Ligne, "to the people who I think like me, and whom I value, for it is impossible for me to run after fine and witty sayings . . . and nothing seems to me to be sillier than what I write when it is to be printed."

There is not, however, in spite of what she says, any distinction to be made between her autograph and other letters. She certainly copied with her own hand the letters addressed to the patriarch of Ferney. And in them all her personal inspiration has certainly its part also, manifesting itself clearly in certain characteristic traits, which belong to her epistolary style, for she has a style of her own : a tone which is familiar, *bon enfant*, a deliberate good-humour, certain originalities of thought or of expression, generally appear even under the turn of phrases most conventionally put together by her usual aids in French and Russian, Shuvalof, Kozitski, or Chrapowiçki.

In her private correspondence, it is mainly the familiar note which prevails, and she is anxious that others should follow her own example. She writes to Peter Saltykof: "Use the familiar and not the ceremonious style in writing to me : I set you the example. I want you also to be in as good a humour in writing to me as I am in writing to you, and that because I care for you a great deal." It is a curious detail that her letters to Saltykof are written in a mixture of French and Russian which she frequently employs, and the passages in which there is the greatest freedom and abandonment are invariably in French. Evidently it is the way of talking in which she is most at home. Her correspondence with Madame Geoffrin shows this, a correspondence which she wishes to set upon a footing of entire familiarity and even equality, for "to have no equals is insupportable," and when the good Parisian gossip finds some difficulty in putting herself in this position, she insists : " Rise, Madame, I do not care for these prostrations ; I have forbidden them . . . My good friend, make use of your opportunities, and tell me quite at your ease whatever you think fit to tell me, without any concern . . . Do not put yourself out, scold me if you like ; I am quite surprised that any one should care to have me for a friend . . . You do not like being contradicted : I will try to accommodate myself to you as far as I can."

She treats Falconet on the same terms : " If you reply, do not put yourself out, do not use any formality, especially do not draw out the epithets which I do not care for in the least . . . You thank me for the confidential tone I have taken with you, but it is for me to thank you for having distinguished me from the number of my *confrères*, who, it is said, are for the most part not suited to be on terms of confidence with people of merit." It is the same with Madame de Bielke : " I was quite struck by the length of time you have known me, twenty-two years ; still, I remember my old friends with the greatest pleasure."

Formerly in the service of the Princess of Zerbst, Catherine's mother, and since then settled at Hamburg, Mademoiselle de Grothus, since her marriage Madame de Bielke, is a German Madame Geoffrin with less intelligence and more curiosity. She too has a salon, but she receives more statesmen than men of letters. She has wide connections, and, especially in regard to the courts of Sweden and Denmark, has at her disposal an abundance of information and anecdote which enables her to enlighten and aid Catherine like a veritable special courier. She listens at doors ; and no doubt, too, people open their ears in her house, and the letters that Catherine sends her are not unknown to the Hanseatic newsmongers who frequent her salon, nor are they intended to be. Hamburg is already one of the most important commercial centres, and besides, at this epoch, a centre of political movement a good deal regarded by the Scandinavian and North German countries. Certainly, faithful to her favourite maxim of "uniting business and pleasure," Catherine sometimes drops into chatting with this "old acquaintance" for the mere love of chatting. When she writes : " I pity the poor Queen of Denmark for having a child-husband ; there is nothing so unpleasant. I know what it is by experience, and I am one of those women who believe that it is always the husband's fault if he is not loved, for, in truth, I should have loved mine if he would only have let me ;" when, in regard to King Christian VII. and his conduct towards Queen Caroline, she observes that "his reign begins to look mightily like that of Peter III.," these confidences are evidently not meant to circulate in the streets of Hamburg. But when she adds the details of a pitched battle won under the walls of Chocim against fifty thousand Turks, the pickers-up of sensational news are certainly thought of, and it is Madame de Bielke's part to make the proper division.

II.

The correspondence of the Semiramis of the North with the patriarch of Ferney has not yet been published in a complete French edition. The Imperial Historical Society has inserted in its *Proceedings*, from 1872 to 1880, a hundred letters of the Empress, addressed to the philosopher, many of which have never been published in France, some in part only, while others are totally different from the texts previously published. This correspondence is, properly speaking, on Catherine's side, a periodical special pleading *pro domo*, an apology in the form of letters for the government and politics of the widow of Peter III., against the criticism and mistrust of a certain portion of the European public. There is even a minute list of the horse-tails taken from the Turkish pashas whom Rumiantsof had routed : " After that, no one can say that that has been bought in the market ! "

The passage in question is one of those not contained in the French editions, and it is highly probable that Catherine herself brought about the omission, as well as all those which she was so anxious to make at the time Beaumarchais took in hand the publication of the master's works, going so far as to request the interference of Louis XVI., and offering to pay for the " cancels " required in making these cuts. The " cancels " were carried out by order of M. de Montmorin, then Minister of Foreign Affairs, but they were never paid for by Catherine.

The letters to Voltaire were, from another point of view, as we know, those which Catherine was accustomed to speak of with the least interest. She confided to Grimm that they were " very vulgarly written." The confession cost her nothing, but she was wrong in looking on them so scornfully, for, for our part, we find some among them that are charming, and in comparison with which even Voltaire's answers gain nothing. The way in which the sovereign from time to time puts down the excesses of adulatory eloquence into which the patriarch is always slipping, is very wittily philosophical, whether it comes from herself or from Shuvalof. Why does he wish to give her a place among the divinities ? Is it so enviable a place, where men have put " onions, cats, the skin of beasts, serpents, and crocodiles " ?

The correspondence between Frederick II. and his somewhat unwilling associate in the partition of Poland, a correspondence in which there is a certain amount of demonstrative cordiality on the part of the King, of reserve on the part of the Empress, is maintained on a footing of official courtesy, in which there is nothing of whim or unconstraint. It is the language of two monarchs talking over their affairs in a friendly way in the presence of their ministers. With Joseph II. it is quite different. In the domain of foreign politics, Frederick II. still remains, but for a few rare exceptions, the representative of the older formal diplomacy. Catherine is quite delighted to meet in Joseph another monarch as saturated as she is with the new spirit, and ready to follow the fashion of the times. This fashion is a certain ease, irony, and lightness in the discussion even of serious questions, all of them qualities which her master, Voltaire, has given her the taste for, which she has adopted with enthusiasm, and which she uses in an indiscriminate feminine fashion, without regard for rule or measure, and utterly indifferent, as we know, to the proprieties. Whether her letters are concerned with small-pox and the inoculation of her grandchildren, or with chasing the Turks from Europe, with the aid of her crowned brother, the tone that she affects, and that he shows himself quite ready to adopt, is the same: light, trifling, *blagueur*, as we should say to-day. While both play their cards warily in regard to the main issues of the affairs, they joke and diverge from the main point, measure their wit against one another, and try to convince each other that they are not only on the level of the great political problems which they are endeavouring to solve together, but also on the level of the most refined intellectual culture ; with mutual flatteries and caresses which it would be difficult to discover in the most hyperbolical compliments of the royal correspondent at Berlin.

We are far from possessing, not only a complete collection of Catherine's correspondence, but even a complete list of her correspondents. In his dispatch of January 31, 1789, to the Comte de Montmorin, the Comte de Ségur refers to one who would otherwise have been quite unknown to us: " I have just discovered, in a secret, but certain, manner, that the Empress has been in correspondence with M. Fox ever since he has been minister." An exchange of letters, at that time, was, in general, merely the expression, as it is to-day, of a social necessity. People did not confine themselves to the communication of news, of ideas, or of business matters ; they wrote for the sake of writing. The Prince de Ligne thus begins one of his letters to Catherine : " If there were only the smallest sort of great man at present existing in the four quarters of the world, I would write to him so as not to trouble you, Madame ; but Your Majesty must needs pay for your own position, and the lack of others." In Germany, Madame de Bielke and Zimmermann, the sovereign's general correspondents, had many lesser rivals ; such as the Baron of Asseburg, who in 1771 was put at the disposal of Catherine by the Danish minister Bernstorff for the negotiation of the marriage of Paul with a German princess. After the fall of Bernstorff, Asseburg, who did not like Struensee, and who had no reason for remaining in Denmark, for he was of Brunswick origin, willingly accepted service in Russia.

Catherine's correspondence with Zimmermann began in connection with the book on *Solitude*, of which the German writer sent her a copy, and which was her favourite reading after the death of Lanskoï. She wrote to him " to talk reason and folly," was enchanted to receive in reply letters " as full of folly as of reason," found that he had, like Diderot, and somewhat like herself, " a mind which goes ahead without knowing where it is going, but always further than any one expects ;" and she tells Grimm of her interest in him, and wishes to get him to come to Russia, like the other great man. But she soon sees that this is something very different from an encyclopædist of Paris. A doctor

by profession, Zimmermann was a German philosopher
and a German savant, and both science and philosophy
in Germany have always had ways of their own.   When
the courier bearing Catherine's first letter and the costly
ring which accompanied it, presented himself at Hanover,
and asked for Dr. Zimmermann, he found the door
closed against him : the doctor was out.

" How unfortunate ! A commission from Her Imperial
Majesty . . . "

" Pardon ! it is Court-Councillor Zimmermann that
you want to see ?   He is in, and will see you."

The messenger has to wait half an-hour ; the coun-
cillor is at his toilet.   He appears at last, in a superb
jacket of silver-cloth.   That was different enough from
the man in black clothes who had been Catherine's
guest ten years before.

The style of his letters does however recall that of
Voltaire's and Diderot's, with a certain heaviness in
addition.   She reads in them that " posterity will be
astonished to see her created and organized for empire,"
and, " aided by her vast genius, making her way to
immortality by all the paths of glory."   She learns also
that her comedies, translated into German, " would be
epoch-making to Europe," and her desire of possessing
so eloquent a man growing yet stronger, she addresses
herself to another German doctor already established in
St. Petersburg, whom we have already seen at Lanskoï's
death-bed.   In similar circumstances, D'Alembert has
shown a fine disdain for the bridge of gold that the
imperial munificence would fain build in his honour ;
Diderot had set out without even knowing if he would

have enough money to last the journey; the German philosopher began by taking precautions, and bargaining. Weickhardt having informed him of Catherine's wishes, he wrote a letter of twenty-seven pages, the point of which was that he would be happy to be near and to serve a sovereign of whom he had the highest opinion, and that he was quite ready to pack up his things, but not without a formal agreement that he was to have an annual allowance of seven or eight thousand thalers at least: the King of England gave him seventeen hundred then, and his patients brought him in three times as much. "You will say that it is too much for a philosopher? My friend, it is too little! I have not yet been able to buy my little plot of land, and the liberty which is the height of my ambition." Besides, Prince Orlof had already proposed to follow him to Russia, offering to establish him "*en Jean-Jacques Rousseau,*" in one of his castles, with ten thousand roubles a year. Zimmermann had refused, and the prince had thrown himself on his neck, weeping tears of regret. As for the princess, she had been half frantic with grief.

"He is very expensive," was Catherine's only comment when she had read the letter, and she dropped negotiations at once. She gave up the physician and merely continued to correspond with the philosopher, touching on all subjects, from the highest moral questions to the making of cheeses. Zimmermann tried to re-open negotiations, on much lower terms; but Catherine thereupon pretended to be very much concerned for the health of the philosopher, for whom she feared the fatigues of so long a journey, and he had to be content

with this honourable defeat. At the time of the Crimean
journey, he wrote to Weickhardt :

"Taurida, Taurida !   That is my first thought when I
awake in the morning, my last when I go to sleep at
night.   On the 4th of January I received from unknown
hands your letter of the 10th December. 'Oh !' thought
I as I unsealed it, 'this letter will be from Taurida.'   Not
a word from Taurida in the letter, but words inexpres-
sibly touching, coming from the most loveliest, greatest,
and most gracious soul that can be found on a throne
or on earth.   Never was there a soul more full of sensibility. 'I cannot decide' (these are her words); 'I made
a decision a year ago, and gave it up, seeing that the
health of your friend might suffer from it.'   These are
the words of an angel.   O God ! such words are the
highest expression of the loftiest, sweetest, and most
touching grace upon earth."

Letters to her relations have also a large place in
Catherine's correspondence.   In these she shows many
amiable qualities.   Her letters to the Grand-Duke Paul
and his wife, during their travels in Europe, are, as far
as the form is concerned, those of a pupil whom Voltaire
has no cause to be proud of, but, in substance, they are
those of a really affectionate mother : "You will please
be good enough all four, father, mother, and two children,
to kiss one another for me," we read in one.   There is
one note among the number, written, for a wonder, in
Russian, of which we must give a translation :

"Alexander Pavlovitch asked me three days ago to
give him another brother.   I send him on to you with
his request, so that you may give him what he asks for.

But I questioned him to know why he wanted one, and
he tells me that he is absolutely in need of a third
brother for the serious reason that he has only one horse
to harness when he plays at horses, and he really ought
to have two.   Feeling that he is entirely in the right, I
hand on his request to you, adding to it what weight
I can on my own behalf.   My dear friend added still
further reasons of the kind, too long to mention in
detail ; it is enough, I hope, for you to know the most
important one."

Charmingly turned, too, with a charming playfulness,
are the letters of the sovereign to Princess Caroline of
Darmstadt, "a robust-minded man, and anything but a
gossip," as Catherine describes her one day to Prince
Volkonski.   Had the friend of Voltaire and of Madame
de Bielke so little taste for gossip ?   The presence of
Grimm in the front rank of her correspondents certainly
seems to prove the contrary.

III.

Grimm is the correspondent *par excellence*.   M.
Schérer's admirably documented book leaves me no
need to acquaint my readers with the curious figure of
this letter-writer and courtier.   I shall merely point out
certain traits, those which seem to me to have caused
him to be chosen by Catherine as the habitual depositary
of her confidences, and in some sort as the daily witness
of her innermost life.

Catherine seems to have figured in 1764 among the

subscribers to the *Correspondance Littéraire.* She found herself well placed : she gave fifteen hundred roubles a year, her *protégé,* the King of Poland, only giving four hundred, and Frederick, whom Grimm took good care not to strike out of his list, nothing at all. During the next few years she turned, more and more frequently, to this man whom she found so well-informed about everything, for the carrying out of various literary and artistic projects ; the purchase of pictures or libraries, the distribution of medals, the colportage of official or unofficial information. She gradually got accustomed to have him at her disposal, and he himself acquired a taste for the post of factotum. When he came to St. Petersburg in 1773, in the suite of the Princess of Hesse-Darmstadt, whose daughter married the Grand-Duke Paul, he was tired of his *Correspondance,* which only brought him in a moderate income, and which he had for some time handed over to Meister. He never for an instant thought of taking up his abode in the Northern capital ; he saw too plainly the double danger of such a course : the certainty of boring himself to death, and the probability of getting sooner or later into disgrace, like his friend Falconet. To stay at Paris, while devoting himself exclusively to the service of the great sovereign, was the object which he had in view, and which he followed up with infinite address. He pleaded his cause in writing, and gave evidence of his particular art, the mixture of seriousness and buffoonery, which had made the fortune of the *Petit Prophète de Boehmischbroda,* as well as the invariable artifice of special pleaders before the great ones of

the earth : parody, and unbounded flattery. He paro-
died the *Credo* in a profession of faith as neophyte in
the "Catherinian" faith, and made use of the English
and German physicians of Her Majesty to translate, in
a burlesque consultation, the idea that he ought to be
sent back to Paris, because he was good for nothing but
writing and doing errands, and that he could only do
so there. He set out, with, as yet, nothing but the
permission to write directly to the sovereign, with a
very small emolument : Catherine had to be economical
just then. But, when he returned in 1776 for the second
marriage of the Grand-Duke Paul, his position was
established. He had audiences which lasted till seven
o'clock, and put the foreign diplomatists on the alert,
the French minister in particular. He became a personage of importance, a position which he did not abuse.
Writing to Madame Geoffrin, he even professed to look
lightly enough on the favour which the Empress showed
him : "She is a charming woman, who ought to live in
Paris ;" but he showed nothing of this in his manner
with the Empress herself. He had adopted in this
particular an attitude from which he never varied to
the end of his life : the attitude of a worshipper absorbed
in the consciousness of his nothingness. If she offered
him the place of director in the new scholastic organization that she had in view, he turned aside the proposal,
saying that he was "tempted to cast himself at her feet,
and beg her to keep him as one of her dogs." He added
moreover that he would be a bad teacher in Russia, as
the language of Voltaire was the only one which he
knew how to use correctly; and then was it not under-

stood that he was always to remain *le rien* of Her
Majesty? This time, when he returned to Paris, he
carried with him the vague, and so all the more attractive,
title of imperial agent, an allowance of two thousand
roubles, and a *tchin* equivalent to the rank of colonel,
which greatly amused Frederick, but in no way disconcerted himself.

He was to see Catherine no more ; yet none the less
he passed, in the eyes of all Europe, and rightly, as the
man who approached her the most closely, living as he
did eight hundred leagues away. He kept this exceptional position for twenty-seven years, receiving in
return certain honorary distinctions, which he esteemed
very highly, and a modest competency, of which the
Revolution deprived him. The Terrorists who pillaged
his house did not discover Catherine's correspondence,
which he had had time to carry into Germany, and had
to content themselves with burning some portraits of
the Empress ; but all he had was lost in the catastrophe.
According to M. Schérer, it was not a confiscation, as
Grimm was a stranger and a diplomatist, doubly protected in this respect by the law of nations ; it was
simply a sequestration, followed by a restitution on the
part of the Executive Council. I would not take upon
myself to contradict the learned biographer, still less to
say anything against the justice of the Revolution ; I
will merely state the facts. The fortune of Grimm, at
the time when it was seized upon by the Revolution,
consisted in thirty thousand livres of annual income, in
addition to somewhat considerable personal effects, and
a fine library. The restitution was only concerned, as

M. Schérer himself admits, with the actual money value. The books, papers, pictures, which escaped the *auto-da-fé*, remained in custody, and some of them have since found their way into the public collections of France. The money value was estimated at sixty thousand livres, and paid in paper-money. The legend of the pair of cuffs, which was all that was ever got out of this payment, and which, as told by Grimm, has the air of being a joke, is only the expression of a very real and very ordinary fact at the time when it occurred. In order to avoid the increasing depreciation in the value of paper-money, the bankers of the imperial confidant had recourse to an expedient common enough in troubled times: they took the money value in goods, and Grimm had for his sixty thousand livres three pairs of lace cuffs and a few pieces of muslin, the whole contained in a box six inches high. This was all that remained to him of the mass of his fortune, after coming in contact with *le bloc révolutionnaire*.

Catherine did something to make up for it by various gifts, intended, according to her expression, "to keep the pot boiling" for her "fag," whose nickname was never more truly deserved. According to her usual custom, she added much more liberal promises, which she forgot to carry out, and the "pot" was not always able to be put over the fire at all. Grimm had a good many mouths to feed. Rather late in life he had come to have quite a family: Emilie de Belsunce, granddaughter of Madame d'Épinay, married to the Comte de Breuil, and the mother of several children, left penniless by the Revolution, and adopted by him. He

handed over all this little flock to Catherine, together
with Antoinette Marchais, a faithful servant who had
courageously, though vainly, defended his house in the
Chaussée d'Antin against its assailants, and who had
followed her master to Germany.   The Empress at first
spoke of receiving them all at St. Petersburg ; but she
was afterwards careful that Grimm should not take her
at her word.   She named him her representative at the
Saxon courts at Gotha, then her resident at Hamburg.
Paul confirmed him in these offices, which, however, the
loss of an eye obliged him to abandon.   He returned to
Gotha, and lived there quietly till 1807, where he died
at the age of eighty-four.   Catherine's letters, which he
had always refused to part from, and which he had
succeeded, through all his troubles, in hiding from view,
were handed over in 1817 to the Emperor Alexander.
They have been published in the *Recueil de la Société
Impériale d'Histoire Russe*, obviously with some omis-
sions.   The letters written by him to the Empress are
not preserved, or are not known, save in fragments.
The copy of the *Correspondance Littéraire* sent to the
illustrious subscriber at St. Petersburg, is in the archives
of Moscow, in a more complete state than the published
text, but with some gaps.

I shall now endeavour to describe this man, whose
life I have summed up from the time when Catherine
had her part in it.   The testimony of his contemporaries
is rarely favourable to him ; that even of Madame
d'Epinay being no exception.   She seems, in her
memoirs, to be pleading a cause which cannot but be
dear to her, but she joins to her pleading the main

points of the indictment, and the effect is somewhat unfortunate. She brings Duclos on the scene, and Duclos declares, straight out, that his former friend, and now rival, is "a cheat, cunning, clever, and insinuating;" recounting his unworthy conduct in regard to "little Fel," the singer whom he looked after so badly, and with Holbach, whose friendship he sought in order "to live with his wife and make use of him as he pleased." Grimm takes his revenge by insinuating to their common friend that Duclos has publicly bragged of her favours, and thereupon Duclos is sent about his business, and Grimm installed as master of the house. Shortly after, Madame d'Épinay is frightened by the discovery of the principles which Duclos' successor puts in practice since he has had to do with crowned heads: "He distinguishes two kinds of justice: one for the use of sovereigns!" It gives her a "mortal" headache. Diderot comes to console her. "I see all that as she does," he writes next day to Mademoiselle Voland; "still, I excuse him as much as I can. At every reproach I add this refrain: But he is young, but he is faithful, but you love him; and she laughs."

The portrait which this necessarily indulgent mistress gives of him is, indeed, that of a painter very much enamoured of his model: "The face is rendered agreeable by a mingling of *naïveté* and *finesse;* the features are interesting, the whole manner negligent and nonchalant; his soul is firm, tender, generous, and lofty. It is just that kind of pride which wins respect without humiliating others. He thinks and expresses himself vigorously, though not with correctness. Badly as he speaks, no

one is listened to more attentively. It seems to me
that in the matter of taste, no one has a finer, surer, and
more delicate sense. He has a turn of pleasantry which
is peculiar to him, and which suits only himself. His
character is a compound of truth, sweetness, savagery,
sensibility, reserve, melancholy, and gaiety. He loves
solitude, and it is easy to see that the taste for society
is not natural to him. No one is more enlightened in
regard to the interests of others, no one gives better
advice, but he does not know how to carry it out."

The taste for solitude, discovered in a person whom
Diderot himself could not help calling "the Marquis," by
way of satire of his vanity and his social pretensions, is
enough to show how much truth there is in the picture ;
and charms discovered in the face whose big prominent
eyes and nose turned awry ("turned always in the right
direction," according to another lady friend) left so
unpleasant an image even in the memory of Meister,
are evidently due to eyes which have been bandaged.
Rousseau perhaps invented the paint which he declares
"the Marquis" used, "to fill the hollows of his skin,"
and the nickname of "Tyran le Blanc" is more probably a recollection of some romance of chivalry which
formed part of Catherine's early reading, than a hit at
this artifice of toilet ; but, physically as well as morally,
the impression conveyed to us by Madame d'Épinay is far
from being that which disinterested observers give us of
the man of whom the Comte de Tilly, for instance, says
in his memoirs that "he would always be in the drawing-
room when he was thought fitter to be in the ante-room,"
and of whom the Paris of the day was mightily amused

when, after going to the funeral of the Comte de Friese, his friend and benefactor, apparently in the deepest distress, his face bathed in tears, he was met a moment after slipping his handkerchief cheerfully into his pocket, and, with an ironical smile on his lips, settling back to the perusal of an interesting pamphlet.

Apart from Diderot, Madame d'Épinay, and two or three other Parisians equally indulgent, Grimm had many acquaintances, but few friends, in the city where he preferred to live and where he wished to die. Paris did not love him, and Paris was not absolutely wrong, for this Frenchman by adoption, this Parisian by predilection, loved neither the city nor the country which he professed to have made his own. *Le Petit Prophète de Boehmischbroda,* which made his literary reputation, is really, at bottom, nothing more nor less than a violent pamphlet against his adopted country: "And I have hidden thy shame and thy falling away from thy neighbours . . . . as though thou hadst not lost the liking of great and fair things, and I have kept them that they should not see thee wallowing in the littleness of thy soul."

Strangers—as it may well be noted in passing by one of themselves—already showed themselves vigorous in rebuking the decadence of France, its disgust of great and fair things, and the narrowness of its ideas, while at the same time they were all equally anxious to come and share in this abasement.

This German looks upon the French language itself, which he uses by preference, as an inferior and ungrateful instrument, to which he refuses even the qualities most commonly accorded to it, clearness and precision. He employs it, one might say, like a bad workman who spits upon his tools. As for the people of the country, they have no merit in his eyes, save for a vivacity which verges upon petulance. German he is, and German he remains, to the inmost fibres of his being. Quite German in his social doctrine: " Shall I tell you what I think? Do not be a child, and afraid of words. I think that there is no other right in the world than the right of the strongest; since that, it must be said, is the only legitimate right . . . To wish that the strongest should not be the master, is almost as reasonable as not to wish that a stone of a hundred pounds should not weigh more than a stone of twenty." And this doctrine leads him to condemn the principle of charity. He urges the suppression of alms-houses, " at the risk of letting those people die in the street who have not managed to provide a support for their old age."

As for Catherine's own opinion in regard to her " fag," it has much the same value as her usual judgments in these matters, half illusion, half *parti pris*. But it is assuredly necessary that we should look, if not for actual qualities, at all events for reasons, and perhaps even defects, which accounted for the choice that she made in this particular case, and the extraordinary confidence, extraordinarily prolonged, which she testified towards this man, whom Duclos continued all his life to call " a scoundrel." These reasons seem to be obvious enough, and made up in equal parts of defects and of qualities.

This German is, in the first place, an honest German.

We shall not try to explain exactly how he managed, with an annual allowance of ten thousand livres, reduced by the changes of currency to seven or eight, and without apparently other sources of income, to have in 1793 an income of thirty thousand livres. But we need not look into that matter more scrupulously than did Catherine herself. In 1795 she sent him ten thousand roubles to distribute among the refugees, forbidding him to say where the money came from, and he rendered a minute account of this apportionment, which was entirely in his own hands. And there is no reason to suppose that he did not do the same with more considerable sums, more than two millions of livres, which from time to time passed through his hands. And he never abused the confidence of Catherine in another respect : guided by an admirable tact, a most delicate sense of things, he never made use of her correspondence in a way of which she could disapprove. She never had to fear a *gaucherie* or an indiscretion on his part. And he was faithful as a dog, keen as a detective, in guarding the secret of the trust confided in him.

He was besides, in regard to the tastes, ways of looking at things, material and moral conveniences of the sovereign, an unrivalled correspondent. " I have never written to any one as I write to you . . . You understand me better than any one, and often the same reflection comes to you at Paris as to me at Moscow. . . . Come, come, M. le Baron, I must have a talk with you. . . . Here are two of your letters waiting to be answered. It is true that there are two from the King of France, three from the King of Sweden, two from

Voltaire, three more from God knows whom, all older in date . . . ; but, as they do not amuse me, because with them I have to write and with you I chatter, . . . I prefer to amuse myself." Coming over and over again in the course of the correspondence, these declarations explain the value which she attached to it. She loves to chatter. She loves, in particular, to write, without need or end, merely to let her pen and her thought run, like piano-players or fencers, who practise on a mute keyboard or at a blank wall. Grimm is her practising keyboard, not however entirely silent ; her practising wall, behind which there is however a sword, a sword properly buttoned, a discreet and respectful sword, but as agile as can be, and provocative of brilliant passages of arms. The habitual tone of the letters which he writes to Catherine is that of constant adulation, almost verging upon folly, with at the same time a perpetual buffoonery, the one playing off against the other, saving the extravagant praise by a semblance of satirical intention, casting a veil of incoherence and fantasy over it all. Hyperbolical flattery, however, with the " fag," is not the mere artifice of a courtier; in time it becomes a second nature to him. He has nothing particular to gain, in the way of either profit or honour, from the Princess of Saxe-Gotha, with whom he gets into correspondence ; still, he can never open one of her letters without " the little shiver that precedes some delightful sensation." He never wearies of kissing her feet, " as the ancients kissed the altar of propitious deities." He does no more with Catherine herself, studying merely to add that element of somewhat gross pleasantry which he knew was so much to her taste. He is equally moved in opening the letters which she writes to him, but his emotion expresses itself differently: he "cries like a calf"; the earthquake at Lisbon is nothing to the shocks which agitate him. A courier from St. Petersburg brings him the portrait of the sovereign, which he has desired to have for so long; he writes: "The revered image has been received with the same ceremony and the same devotion as that with which Count Suvorof receives an order of St. André at Kinburn; except that I have not taken the sacrament, I can flatter myself that I have laughed, wept, and behaved as much like a madman as he. Why have I not taken both sacraments, like him, before touching the revered image! . . Blessed be she who, full of grace, has deigned to confer upon her 'fag' this priceless image of the immortal one."

At the same time he is quite content to be addressed in the same jocose way, and even at his own expense, to be turned into ridicule in regard to his personal appearance and his private character, his wit and his health, his intestinal derangements, and his aristocratic pretensions. Is he not the "fag"? He is also "George Dandin," "M. l'Hérétique," "Heraclitus," "M. le Freiherr," "L'Homme aux boyaux fêlés." And it is not Catherine only who is allowed to jest with him after this fashion: Frederick calls him M. de la Grimmalière "since he has become baron, and he does not appear to mind in the least." But (and here his art, his superiority comes in) he does not limit himself to taking blows, which would soon become insipid, he knows how to venture, at the right moment, in replies, and even bold attacks, but which only amuse without wounding, so clever is he in wrapping up the point. In sending to the Empress the model of a monumental gate designed by Clérisseau, he writes: " Now I trust that Your Majesty will not see fit to have a German quarrel with me over this model gate, nor say to me, ' I fear that it is too beautiful,' for I shall be quite capable of printing Your Majesty's letter. Now such a publication would do no little wrong to the Empress, for the universe would then perceive that there are sometimes such hubbubs in Your Majesty's interior that one knows not what to listen to, that ideas jostle one another, fall over each other topsy-turvy, so that it needs all the German phlegm of a ' fag ' not to be sent sprawling."

These little revolts are easily forgiven, especially as he knows how to excuse himself with all the humility of which he is capable, and his capacity in this respect is infinite: it is that of " an earthworm which, despite the tone of lightness which it sometimes permits itself in its excess of gaiety . . . never forgets its origin, that is to say its nothingness." They are welcomed, indeed, for they arouse and excite his august correspondent. She needs them to set her fancy flying, and her pen, heaping up puns and jokes and sarcasms, gay frolickings of a mind which jumps at one leap from politics to the scandals of the ante-room, from philosophy to incongruity. The mere thought of talking with the " fag " puts her in a gay mood, and adds a certain drollery even to the headings of her letters: " From the once duck-pond, now St. Petersburg ;" " separate

sheet to be thrown into the fire without losing it ;" "at
Peterhof, where neither I nor M. Thomas are on good
terms with one another" (M. Thomas being Her
Majesty's favourite dog). And then the endless nicknames! Not a single creature is called by his right
name ; things themselves take on strange disguises.
Joseph II., before the meeting at Mohilef, is "the man
with two faces," or the *piccolo bambino ;* after, he
becomes "the eagle." Maria Theresa is " Mamma."
" Falstaff" stands for Gustavus III. of Sweden. We
know already who she means in speaking of "poor
folk." " Pea-soup" is meant to take off the diplomatists ; and, in laughing at the anarchic revolution-
aries she writes : *die Köther Bärenhäuter,* or *Bärenreiter,*
commenting on this last as follows : "In Pomerania it
is a dirty, ugly dog that one calls *Köther* . . . I
cannot see that *Bärenhäuter,* one who wears bear-
skin, is any insult, but a man who rides on a bear is
ridiculous."

Note that these nicknames are not meant to be any
sort of cryptograms, the " budgets " to Grimm not being
exposed to the accidents of the post. It is mere fun
and foolery. She caricatures the very language in
which she writes, employing a patois of her invention,
a mixture of French, German, and Italian locutions,
which all bear her sign-manual. She says that the war
has " déprojeté ses projets." She announces that to-
morrow "elle legislatera." She writes : " Ma si il signor
marchese del Grimmo volio fare mi plaisir." And she
comes and goes, full speed, winding as best she can,
through all these freaks and follies, the infinite skein of

her imagination. She sometimes even calls the "fag" her skein-winder.

She is grateful to him too, poor man, for a place that she comes to take, not only considerable, but, in course of time, unique, in his existence and her thoughts. The history of the relations of Grimm with his imperial friend is the history of the gradual and finally complete absorption of one individuality by another. He is conscious of it himself: "This correspondence has become the only good, the single ornament, of my life, the pivot of my happiness, as essential to my existence as breathing . . . I came to have for her, at a distance, a kind of religion which was all made up of her and the worship I rendered to her. The thought of her had become so habitual with me that it never left me day or night, and all my thoughts were wrapt up in this one . . . Walking, travelling, visiting, sitting, lying, standing . . . my whole existence had come to be, as it were, concentrated in hers." Moreover, this communion of spirits came to isolate him from the outer world. He gave up reading, he who had once been *Correspondance Littéraire*. He writes to the Empress, carries out her commissions, receives people on her account, writes to her again; and there is all his life. Finally, the German in him appearing once more under the varnish of French education, as the man of letters that he had become in France gives place to the courtier, he comes to interest himself vaguely in the literary movement beyond the Rhine. But what a choice he makes! He echoes Catherine in putting the Thummels and Schlummels on the same level as Voltaire; with her, he dis-

covers an " incredible vigour " in the comedies of Lenz,
and, like her, does not seem to doubt that *Goetz von
Berlichingen, Werther,* and *The Robbers,* have already
appeared, and that German romanticism is already born.

The secret of this extraordinary monopoly in possession of a whole soul, Catherine is well aware of. She
knows that, at bottom, it is nothing very flattering
either for her or for him. She does not fail to joke her
" fag " about it ; quite aware " that he is never happier
than when he is by, near, beside, before, or behind, some
Highness ! " and God knows " where he picks them
up ! " He even jests about it himself, telling of his
appearance in a box of the theatre at Spa, in company
with Joseph II. and Prince Henry of Prussia, and his
pleasure in fancying what an effect it would have on
the gossips of the place, who would have to confess
" that, in truth, the fag of a Greek Imperial Majesty
must, all the same, be a creature of some distinction ! "
She does not endeavour to raise him above the level
where he has set himself, and where he seems so much
at home. He is quite justified in denying that he has
ever played the part of a more or less underhand agent
of imperial politics at Paris. Once only, in 1789, at
a time when the official and diplomatic *personnel* of the
French Government has fallen into great disorder, the
Empress gives him a commission of this kind, and he
does not gain enough out of it to make him at all
anxious to try it over again. " Fag " he wished to be,
and " fag " he will remain ; of too conceited a humour
to be content with a place in the republic of letters ; of
too vain and too light a disposition, also, to engage in

really serious affairs, while taking up a position in the highest spheres of the society of the time. His mind and character, his very nature, condemn him to positions of inferiority. He might have been a writer, but prefers to be a reporter. Catherine might very likely have made him a minister : he insists on being nothing but a factotum. A sort of servility creeps into even his most brilliant and solid qualities. He seems born in the ante-room, and home-sick for livery. Like the lackey who made a fortune out of Law's speculations, though he is in a position to ride inside his coach, his instinct urges him to get up behind. He was, however, an excellent man in his way. It has been said that, having wished to find a place among the Empress's dogs, he did not fail to bark at the Revolution. This is rather a hard saying, and, at all events, it was not the Revolution which suffered, and there were certainly reasons for his not being too amiably disposed towards it. But he was not naturally inclined to be malicious. To posture before his Empress, and to amuse her by his posturings, was enough for him.

It was doubtless on account of just these qualities that Catherine was what she was to him, and that she thus added to her other titles to fame that of having left a unique model of her particular kind of epistolary style, and an autobiographical document which is unrivalled. In the fortunes of her career, Grimm was one good fortune the more.

CHAPTER III.

CONFIDENTIAL AGENTS.—PRINCESS DASHKOF.

I.

GREAT man as Catherine was, according to Voltaire, she was also, in certain respects, very characteristically feminine. Something of the kind is to be seen in the singular number of her confidential friends, dubious enough figures, whose official functions are doubled by another less avowable one. All through her reign, the Empress indulges in confidential missions to an enormous extent. But (and here it is that Catherine the Great comes upon the scene with all the masculine vigour of her genius and her will) great as is the number of the men and women whom she uses as confidential agents, there is not a single one of them, man or woman, who succeeded in reversing the parts. She makes use of them ; never do they make use of her. This trait is seen very clearly in the history of the most famous woman whom she had about her.

In 1773, writing to Frederick II. in regard to the difficulty of influencing Catherine in favour of the new notions as to the King of Poland, Solms writes : " I have knocked at every door ; the women, on this occasion, have been utterly useless. This is not the age of women in Russia." In the presence of a woman on the throne of Peter the Great, in succession to Elizabeth, Anne, and Catherine I., the statement is curious. Certainly the Princess Dashkof could never have dreamt of such a thing on the day when, dressed in the same grenadier's uniform, she galloped with her imperial friend on the way from St. Petersburg to Peterhof in chase of a crown. But her dreams were doomed to deception, and it only needed a day to prove the truth of what Solms had stated : the triumph of Catherine was not that of her devoted friend, and, only a few weeks after the accession of the new Empress, the companion of her hours of ordeal had lost even her prerogatives as keeper of the imperial conscience, which she had hoped at least to retain for herself. Her part was ended.

It is but just to say that she behaved in an absolutely insupportable manner. With her eighteen-years-old inexperience, her quarrelsome humour, and her ambition, she soon gave evidence of the most fatal qualities of a busybody. She wanted to order everything and everybody, she gave instructions to the soldiers, placed and unplaced officials, and took the high hand with Catherine herself. She pretended to be unwilling to accept a decoration that was offered to her, and made it understood that she had expected the office of a minister or the command of a regiment. She pocketed the twenty-four thousand roubles which were allotted to her among the rewards, but pretended that it was a mere nothing to what she had reason to expect, and wearied every one with her lamentations. " Princess Dashkof," wrote Béranger to the Duc de Praslin, " has lamented to me over the little she has made out of the Revolution. I blushed for her in silence, hearing her thus shamelessly enlarge upon her poverty and her disgrace."

Catherine could not be expected to agree to a sharing of power, and the " French-speaking Thomyris," as Voltaire called her, aimed at nothing less. Thus no understanding was possible between the two former friends. Those who took the princess's place were merely ante-room confidantes, without political import-ance or desire after it. She herself languished for seven years in the neighbourhood of the court, woefully disap-pointing those foreign diplomatists who had counted upon her favour, not even succeeding in being taken seriously in her threatening airs and pretences of revolt. Her share in the plot of Mirovitch in 1764, and the risk she is supposed to have run of being put to the torture, do not seem to us proved. " Her romantic and super-ficial disposition," wrote Solms in 1763, " is so well known that there is no likelihood of many people enter-ing upon any enterprise in her company." She did not dispute, she " wrangled," as Grimm said of her later on. In 1769 she expressed a desire to travel, received a bag containing four thousand roubles, and these words, written by the Empress in pencil : " For the post-horses," at which she wept with rage, but pocketed the money, and set out.

She visited Paris, where Diderot saw her and became

enthusiastic over her, in his usual way ; London, where she met Paoli, and was disgusted to find him in receipt of a pension from the King of England ; then Italy, where she expressed great admiration for the pictures and statues, which she professed to discover. On her return to Russia she took up once more her attitude of unwilling victim. In order to be quit of her it occurred to Catherine in 1782 to appoint her directress of the Academy of Arts and Sciences. She flatly refused : " Make me directress of your washer-women," she said to the Empress at a court ball. Returning home, still in her ball-dress, she wrote a long letter, giving the reasons for her refusal, and, in the middle of the night, rushed off and awakened Patiomkin, whom she found in his bed (the recent advent of Lanskoï having afforded him some leisure), in order to ask him to hand on her letter to the Empress. He read the letter, tore it up without a word, and went to sleep again. She returned home and took up her pen again. By seven in the morning she had finished another letter more virulent than the first, obstinately refusing the office which was to be conferred upon her : she had not yet taken off her ball-dress. At last she went to bed. When she awoke, the imperial ukase calling her to her new duties lay beside her bed. She put on a more tragic air than usual, and presided over the academy. In the following year, she wanted to preside over two, an idea having occurred to her for a Russian Institute. Catherine let her carry out her plan. " She has no time to worry over things now, for she has a good big morsel in her mouth which keeps her jaws active," she wrote to Grimm.

The lady-president showed great zeal in the exercise of her double duties, and effected several useful reforms. The art-gallery which she endeavoured to put on a European footing was very curiously composed. Among other objects exposed to the admiration of visitors were two glass jars filled with spirits of wine in which were preserved two heads decapitated by order of Peter I., one of which had belonged to Moëns, the son of a Flemish jeweller established at Moscow, brother of that Anna Moëns who preceded Catherine I. in the affections of the terrible Emperor. He had become the lover of the Tsarina, and was denounced, it is said, by Iagoujinski to the vengeance of the Tsar. The other was that of Lady Hamilton, who was guilty of having yielded to the Tsar's desires, and became *enceinte* in consequence. Peter had his own ideas in regard to expiatory justice. He ordered the child to be destroyed and the mother decapitated. The two heads had been in the museum since 1724. Princess Dashkof had them removed. In 1786 she had a new map of Russia made by one of her academies. "This map, announced with such a flourish of trumpets," wrote the Comte de Ségur to M. de Vergennes, "has been severely criticized. It is found to be no more exact than the others. Only the northern part and Siberia and the part lying towards America are better given, because they are copied from Cook, who has cut down the imaginary possessions of Russia by two or three degrees."

We have related elsewhere the disputes of the lady-president and the Empress in literary matters, disputes which ended in 1784 in the suppression of the journal published under the auspices of the former. Ten years later, another quarrel of the same kind suppressed the lady-president's functions altogether. She had given her authorization and aid to the printing of a posthumous tragedy of Kniajnin (*Vadim at Novgorod*), which was not to the Empress's taste. Catherine had the publication suppressed, and the princess wiped out the affront by sending in her resignation. She quitted St. Petersburg to take up her abode at Moscow, and the last meeting of the two friends of long ago was far from being a friendly one. Introduced after an hour of waiting, the princess bowed in silence. "Bon voyage, madame," said the Empress. That was all.

The opinion of contemporaries is for the most part little sympathetic to this *déclassée* of politics, who seems to lead the way to the *femmes incomprises* of the following century. Castera even accuses her of having trafficked in Italy with an influence she did not possess, drawing upon artistes whom she promised to recommend to the opulent Semiramis of the North. Thiébault attributes a droll motive to the hasty fashion in which she left Paris. Finding herself surrounded in a public promenade by a group of curious persons, she accosted a knight of the Order of Saint-Louis.

"Why do you consider me like that?"

"Madame, I look at you, but I do not consider you."

She rushed through the crowd furiously, hastened home, called for horses, and set out without giving herself the time to take her son with her, who had to follow her to England.

Diderot has nothing to say of this adventure, and

the portrait that he paints of the princess, very unattractive from the physical point of view, is, from the
moral point of view, coloured with all kinds of charms,
such as only lovers know how to lend to their models.
She has audacity, and she "feels things proudly." He
finds in her a profound sentiment of "honesty and
dignity," a profound knowledge of the men and affairs
of her nation, a decided aversion to despotism, penetration, *sang-froid*, and judgment, modesty even, "to
the point of not allowing one to admire her," a trait
which, as applied by the amiable painter, is common to
the princess and to Catherine, and seems in both cases
about equally near the truth. Is he really in love, this
eternal enthusiast? He is positively jealous of his
princess. He comes to see her every day, "at night-
fall," when she returns from her visits all over Paris, to
talk with her "of what is not to be seen : laws, customs,
administration, finances, politics, manners, arts, sciences,
letters, nature," and also doubtless to gain a closer
knowledge of "this soul dogged by misfortune." And
he will not let any one else share this privilege. Sometimes he hinders the noble stranger from accepting an
invitation to supper at Madame Necker's, "where she
will not be esteemed at her true worth," sometimes he
prevents her from meeting Rulhière. He is even chary
of good Madame Geoffrin ! The princess insists a little
in regard to Rulhière, who has written a book which
interests her somewhat closely. But he points out to
her that "she will admit various things, without contradicting them, and that he will not fail to take advantage of her testimony." She once more resigns herself,

and kisses her mentor, which seems greatly to delight him, in spite of the "fat lips" and "bad teeth" that he attributes to his friend.

Miss Wilmot, the future depositary of the memoirs of the princess, is not likely to be more impartial. The silhouette, however, which she draws with her pen in writing to her parents from the country near Moscow, whither she has followed her friend, is quite that of the bustling, troublesome, and difficult person, whom other witnesses have shown us at St. Petersburg, and not the one whom Diderot fancied he saw at Paris. The model has aged (the princess is now over sixty), but without undergoing any very great transformation : "Whatever she does, she is different from any one else ; not only have I never seen, but I have never even heard of such a being. She shows the masons how to build houses, helps to make shirts, to milk the cows, plays, writes for the press, knows the Church services from A to Z, and corrects the Pope if he does not say the prayer as he ought. She knows by heart all the plays that they act, and corrects the actors if they make a mistake. She is physician, apothecary, surgeon, farrier, carpenter, judge, monk . . . She corresponds with her brother, who occupies one of the highest places in the empire, with men of learning and of letters, and also with dirty Jews, out of whom she hopes to make something. She manages to write at the same time to her son, to various relations, to all her family. Her conversation, attractive by its simplicity, falls sometimes into an infantile *naïveté*. She unconsciously speaks French, Italian, and Russian all jumbled together. She gets to a ball two hours before the candles are lit, and insists on her friends accompanying her."

This is more like the princess in *ski* or in *of* whom we see to-day, carrying her stormy eccentricity across Europe, "the first appearance of the Russian woman in history," according to Herzen, at all events of the Russian woman escaped from the restraints of a home, and rushing about over Europe, in whom the modern nervosity of the feminine temperament seems to meet with its most complete representative. It would be sad for Russia if it had only this type of wife, mother, or even of blue-stocking; all the more so as the real feeling of the Russian mind in regard to this "historic apparition" is, if possible, less favourable even than that of other nations. The brother of the princess, A. R. Vorontsof, accuses her of having behaved very badly to her sister, the unhappy favourite of Peter III., taking advantage of her disgrace, at the time of the victorious *coup d'État* of Catherine, to appropriate her belongings. All her life she is on somewhat bad terms with her relations. We can excuse her so far as her father is concerned, for he was a gross, savage, and sordid personage, notorious for his greed, and his scorn of all kinds of culture: his singular hatred of electricity has passed into a legend. Her son, too, is but a clown and a drunkard, but he is also the product of an education whose responsibility is entirely hers. When he is thirteen, she announces to Robertson that she has already made him one of the most learned men in Europe, and she sends a long list of the various kinds of knowledge which she has instilled into him. Later on, in the same town and almost under the same roof with him, she refuses to go to his death-bed. She is also on the worst of terms with her daughter, who, always in debt and difficulties, prefers poverty to the task of living with her mother. She disputes with all the world. Her disagreements with her neighbour, Léon Naryshkin, which lead, in 1788, to a ridiculous trial *à propos* of pigs, has become celebrated. Catherine turned it into a little comedy, *Za mouhoï s'abouhom* (A Hammer to Kill a Moth), and Naryshkin pretended to find in her pimpled cheeks the blood of the pigs she had slaughtered. The disinterestedness to which she lays claim in her memoirs is anything but founded on fact. She takes Catherine's gifts, it is true, with disdain, but she frequently asks for more. She affects also a great contempt for the favourites, but she finds means to come to terms with one of them in regard to an estate which the Empress has given her, on which she does not find the stated tale of heads. She has liberal ideas, but she grinds down her peasants, and flogs them with implacable severity. In order to obtain her permission to follow a lover outside her domains, a poor girl has to pay her a sum of a hundred roubles. As she grows older, she acquires the most sordid avarice ; she unharnesses the horses of those who come to see her in her *datcha* near the capital, and employs them in her garden ; taking advantage of the fashion of *parfilage*, which exists then in the St. Petersburg salons, she lays hold of all the bits of gold thread that she finds on the tables, and sells them without compunction. Dobrynin mentions in his memoirs a house belonging to the princess, in which he lived while he was at Moscow, and which was supposed to have been built with the funds of the Academy of Sciences.

In spite of all this, her memory was lately celebrated in a solemn gathering of the learned assembly. But the memory of Catherine deserves also to be defended against the imputation of injustice and ingratitude, which one might be tempted to make on the strength of the princess's memoirs, where a few eulogies, brought in with a sort of orator's artifice, do but little to veil the vindictive animosity of the writer.

" I cannot accommodate myself to everybody," said Catherine one day to Chrapowiçki, speaking of her former friend. " As for her, she could not get on with any one."

II.

In 1773, at the very time when Solms was so deeply regretting his inability to get at some feminine influence at the court of Catherine, the sovereign had indeed one female friend and confidante, but one who could be of no use. " The Empress is on familiar terms only with the Countess Bruce, and the Countess never dares talk to her of affairs," declared the diplomatist. There were certain affairs indeed on which the Countess Bruce was in communication with the Tsarina, but which had no interest either for Frederick or his envoy. It is only fair to say that Princess Dashkof would probably not have concerned herself with these affairs. The Countess Bruce concerned herself with them for many years, to the entire satisfaction of her imperial friend, up to the time when it happened to her, as we have related, to forget herself in the exercise of her duty. Catherine was merciful. Korsakof was a handsome man, the part played by the Countess necessarily brought about, between her and the imperial favourites, a somewhat dangerous intimacy, and the Empress could not be so very greatly surprised if she acquired an after-taste for those merits and charms which she had had the opportunity of appreciating before. The confidante merely followed the favourite into exile, where she was abandoned by him in her turn. Catherine always kept an indulgent recollection of her. "It is impossible not to regret her when one has known her so well," she wrote to Grimm in 1785, on hearing the news of her death. The confidential attributes of the Countess, in regard to which we find it a little difficult to be quite explicit, were at one time the object of very numerous and very definite commentaries. Byron has sung them in a celebrated stanza, describing the first appearance of Don Juan at the court of Catherine, where the Countess Bruce was then replaced by Mademoiselle Protassof:

> " An order from her Majesty consign'd
>   Our young lieutenant to the genial care
> Of those in office : all the world look'd kind
>   (As it will look sometimes with the first stare,
> Which youth would not act ill to keep in mind),
>   As also did Miss Protassof then there,
> Named, from her mystic office, 'l'Éprouveuse,'
> A term inexplicable to the Muse."

The Countess Bruce is a sister of the great Ru-

miantsof ; her husband does not live with her, for which
he may be excused, but this does not hinder him from
profiting by her position in order to raise himself,
without other merit, to a high situation.   The son of a
Scotchman who came to Russia during the protectorate
of Cromwell, he becomes senator, general-in-chief, lieutenant-colonel of the Siemonovski Guards, and finally
governor-general of Novgorod and of Twer, in the place
of Sievers.

After the catastrophe of 1779, we are assured by
Harris that Catherine shifts her confidence to one of the
Engelhardt ladies, though it is impossible to imagine,
without further proof, that she took up the "mystic"
and inexplicable heritage of the Countess, to which her
character, so far as we know of it, seems utterly alien.
This niece of Patiomkin has also passed for a daughter
of the sovereign and of the favourite.   This has been
brought forward as an explanation of her privileged position in the imperial retinue ; she was lodged at the palace,
treated with the utmost affection, and provided with a
train worthy of a princess of the blood royal.   There is
nothing to justify this supposition, and the exceptional
favour which she enjoyed can be explained on another
supposition.   In 1781 she becomes, by her marriage
with Count Braniçki, the wife of the last *Grand Général*
of Poland, and as such this confidante (who for several
generations set the example of all the virtues, revered
by her children and grandchildren, adored as a good
fairy by her peasants in the Ukraine) has, for her imperial friend, a particular merit : she becomes, at the
time of the final partition of the Republic, an expressive

personification of the work of conquest and assimilation on the banks of the Vistula. In 1790, Catherine even gives her a certain political position : a letter addressed to her by the Empress, which is reproduced in the *Gazette de Hambourg*, and much circulated in Poland, is intended to recall the Poles to reason, carried away just now by a burst of heroic resistance to the foreign invasion, and to counsel them "not to imitate the nightingale, who, singing with eyes shut, let itself be swallowed by a toad," a comparison which one would think more ingenious than flattering to the person who employs it.

As for Mademoiselle Protassof, who, from 1781, figures on the list of confidantes ordinary and extra-ordinary, there is no reserve to be made ; she enters directly upon the heritage of Countess Bruce, and her position is universally recognized. A near cousin of the Orlofs, the daughter of a "show" senator, she adds to her other duties that of spy, exercised by means of Mademoiselle Nelidof, the ungrateful and treacherous favourite of Paul. Born in 1744, she survives Catherine many years. She is present at the Congress of Vienna, covered with diamonds like a reliquary, and claiming precedence over every one ; doubtless on the strength of having gone before Catherine under other circumstances.

As for Anna Naryshkin (born Princess Trubetzkoï), at whose house, as early as 1755, the rendezvous of the Grand-Duchess with Poniatowski used to take place, her part in Catherine's intimacy and in the history of favouritism seems to have been that of a wary and discreet courtier, not forgetful of her perquisites. Zubof, immediately after his rise to the post of favourite, presents her with a valuable watch, and that, doubtless, is not all she gains by it. For a long time Catherine could not be without her. In the rare cases when she was absent from the palace, where she always had her suite of rooms, affectionate and pressing messages were soon sent, begging her to come back as soon as possible: "As I know that you are a most charitable lady, that you visit the sick and the dead, at the expense of your health, I hope that you will extend your good works to me. I have fallen sick, and am ready to receive extreme unction; were it only for the sake of seeing you, I would have it given to me. Deign, then, to honour me with your visit, if blood-letting and purges, washings and sudorifics, do not confine you to the house. Come at once, despite the fog and the bad weather; come, if only to make Guyon (the court physician) laugh, for he witnesses the testament that I send you. And do not forget to bring something to make me laugh, for when one is taking purges, one is always melancholy."

Anna Naryshkin died in 1820 in the house of her cousin, Rumiantsof, Catherine's envoy to the refugees at Coblenz, whom the childless widow had gone to keep company.

I am sorry to associate with these dark and dubious figures that of a woman who won the confidence of the Empress on entirely different grounds, a confidence which became veneration on the part of Catherine's successors. Madame de Lieven ought not to be included in this chapter; but it would be difficult to find a place for her elsewhere. She has a place apart in the retinue of Catherine, a unique place.

A certain de Lieven was the most faithful follower of Charles XII. Political vicissitudes, which had made his native country a Russian province, had impoverished the family, formerly one of the wealthiest in Livonia. Charlotte de Lieven (*née* de Posse) was the wife of a major-general in the service of Russia, and was living quietly in a suburb of Riga, bringing up her four children on the scanty resources of a small income, when she was recommended to Catherine by Sievers for the education of Paul's daughters. She was terrified at the idea of leaving her retreat, and of entering upon all the perils of a court which, alike in all she knew and all she did not know of it, was equally formidable in her eyes. But Brown, the governor of the district, received orders which he carried out as Catherine's orders were generally carried out : put into a carriage, almost by force, Madame de Lieven was hurried off to St. Petersburg, taken straight to the palace, and brought before one of Her Majesty's secretaries, who had orders to examine her. He questioned her, and, half dead with fatigue and anxiety, she could but tell her trouble, the grief it had been to her to leave her children, and the longing she had to go back to them again. She was pouring out her story, when a hard and curt feminine voice, softened by a kindly inflexion, interrupted her :

" You are the woman I want ! Come with me."

The Empress had drawn aside a curtain without her perceiving it, and stood before her.

This was in 1783. Since then, Madame de Lieven

lived for nearly half a century at the court which had
so greatly alarmed her. She looked after the education
of the Grand-Duchesses, and even of the Grand-Dukes,
Catherine's grandsons, " with a sometimes brutal frankness," says Guizot, who was a friend of her daughter-in-
law, the famous Princesse de Lieven, but with the most
accomplished skill. Paul, who had never found a mother
in Catherine, centred all the respect and a little of the
affection for which he could find no other outlet, upon
the governess of his children. Alexander and Nicholas
looked upon her as their grandmother. She died in
1828, after having been raised to the rank of princess
and highness in 1826, at the coronation of the second of
her pupils.

III.

According to a tradition, very generally accepted in
Russia, the place which belongs to Ivan Ivanovitch
Betzki is not merely that of the principal confidant of
Catherine, but something much higher. Gretch speaks
of the striking resemblance between the Empress and
this supposed father, and the portrait of a daughter of
Ivan Ivanovitch in the possession of M. M. O. Ribas, at
Odessa, certainly carries out this statement. I cannot
say if the Empress really was accustomed, as it has
been stated, to kiss the hand of this enigmatic personage; but it is certain that she showed him an affection
and deference which might easily be taken for filial
piety ; that she frequently went to see him, even before
his age had put it out of his power to respond to

her summons, and that she would stay and dine with him without ceremony, which she did with no one else.

The natural son of Prince Ivan Trubetzkoï and a Swede, the Countess Wrede, Betzki was twenty-six years of age when, in 1728, he became an *attaché* of the Legation at Paris, where he met the Princess of Anhalt-Zerbst. He returned to the capital of the intellectual world in 1755, and made other acquaintances, which had an equally important influence on his ultimate career. Welcomed by the encyclopædists, an intimate of Madame Geoffrin's salon, he knew Diderot, who initiated him into matters of art, and Rousseau, whose educational views he adopted. He thus became, on his return to Russia, a sort of oracle in regard to all questions concerned with that domain of superior culture with which he had found himself in contact. A medal, which was struck later on, represents him on one of its sides, with his somewhat heavy profile, whilst on the other there is a figure of Gratitude, with its ordinary attributes, clasping a pyramid on which a medallion bearing his cipher is attached by four children representing the four establishments which he founded or re-organized: the Foundling College, the National Gallery, the Corps des ·Cadets, and the Convent of Smolna. All these establishments were under his control. He professed also to take under his control the intellectual and artistic movement connected with them. In this he showed, as Falconet's misadventures prove, more authoritativeness than tact or intelligence. He liked people of talent to be docile. He professed also to love France, admitting that the man whom he called "the friend or rather the gossip of Catherine" was " not a bad sort of man," " enjoying absolute power in the little matters in which he is concerned." Sabatier adds : " He had a weakness for us, which he sacrificed to his position."

His natural daughter, who bore so strong a resemblance to Catherine, was that Anastasia Sokolof whom Diderot was so delighted to meet in Catherine's ante-room. Always gay and sparkling, she amused Catherine by her stories of her adventures in Paris, where she had accompanied Princess Galitzin, and by the letters (which are described as " dull and moral," by the Marquise de Beausset in one of his dispatches to the Duc de Praslin) which she received from Mademoiselle Clairon, from whom she had taken lessons in declamation. She married the adventurer Ribas, whom Catherine raised to the rank of admiral, and from a mere lady-in-waiting became one of the most trusted friends and most valued confidantes of the sovereign.

Betzki died in 1795. The little obituary that Catherine made of him in her correspondence with Grimm, does not show the trace of any emotion, however veiled, which corresponds in any way with the hypothesis of parentage to which we have alluded : " This 31st August, after dinner, M. Betzki has just died, about two hours since, at the age of ninety-three. It is nearly seven years since he sunk into a state of senility, almost of idiotcy. For the last ten years he has been blind. When any one came to see him he said, ' If the Empress asks you what I am doing, tell her that I

am working with my secretaries.' He hid himself
away from me on account of his loss of sight, for fear
that I should deprive him of his offices. As a matter
of fact, they had all been filled up, but without his
knowledge."

Betzki is in some sort an intermediary between the
new Russia, the Russia of Peter I. and Catherine II.,
and the Western world. From this point of view, he
forms the complement to Grimm, as from another point
of view Grimm's place is taken by Chrapowiçki. He is
the standing "fag," the factotum always at hand,
similarly employed for local commissions, tormented
like the other, and treated with the same mixture of
kindness and of somewhat contemptuous familiarity.
She jokes him about his corpulence, and advises him to
use a sofa rather than a chair as a seat, "for if he were
to fall, he could never get up again"; she asks him if
his legs are not tired after he has been running about
on her errands; if he has not quarrelled with his lady-
love, when he looks sad; she apologizes to him for an
outburst of impatience; hits him in the ribs with a roll
of paper, and even asks him to stay to dinner, "since he
is there." He takes it all with the same placidity, and
notes everything in his journal, which reads as if it had
been made by a phonograph, and which is an invaluable
document for the private history of Catherine.

Of Polish origin, the son of one of the gentlemen-
guards of the Empress Elizabeth, grandson on his
mother's side of a confidant of Peter I., whose wife,
Helen Serdiakof, was supposed to be the daughter of
the great Tsar, he has every opportunity for making

his way in the world; but, after an honourable beginning, both in the army and the magistracy, and some
attempts in the direction of literature, he slips, like
Grimm, into a position of dependence. Fat and scant
of breath as he is, he exhibits in his official duties the
agility of a deer and the flexibility of an earth-worm.
The exact opposite of the Princess Dashkof, he is on
good terms with every one; with Patiomkin and with
the Orlofs, with Bezborodko and Viaziemski. He gets
on marvellously well with the favourite of to-day, and
knows beforehand who will be the favourite of to-
morrow. It is thus that he makes a friend of Mamonof
before Catherine has ever noticed the *red coat.* Dissolute, and far from squeamish in his tastes, he frequents
all the low resorts of the capital, and frequently runs
the risk of serious encounters. One morning some one
who has come to ask a favour is taken aback at seeing
on his face the marks of the blows which he had given
him in a tavern-quarrel over-night, without knowing who
he was. Chrapowiçki, however, receives his boisterous
adversary in a perfectly friendly way. He is a good
honest fellow, and Catherine considers him to be incor-
ruptible, so as to wager her hand that he does not
take any *vziatki*, or tips, which is perhaps going too
far. In any case, he is discreet, indefatigable, and
punctual. He only gets drunk on those days when he
is sure of not being required by Her Majesty, and, in
case of surprise, he has recourse, with equal success, to
the energetic measures found so efficacious by Bezborodko. He has no opinions of his own in regard to
anybody or anything. His journal does not even tell

us what he thinks of Catherine. Perhaps he has no opinion even of her. He is content to register the slightest words and actions, and he knows, too, how to make her speak. Like Grimm, he "winds the skein" of her thought. And, like him, he has the gift of inexhaustible and cunning flattery, unwearied and unwearying. But the journal which he keeps in secret becomes the rock on which his fortune finally breaks. Catherine has no desire of going down to posterity by so confidential a medium, and, betrayed no doubt by something which he says during one of his drunken fits, he denies the fact with the utmost effrontery, but in vain; he is quietly set aside, in some honorary position as senator. He dies in 1801, a few months after the death of Paul I.

His predecessor had been a native of Little Russia, Kozitski, the son of the pope of Kief, where he had been brought up in the ecclesiastical college; a learned Greek and Latin scholar, and a distinguished man of letters. When Patiomkin comes into power, he has a momentary fit of aberration: believing himself lost on account of his connection with the Orlofs, he cuts his throat. He recovers, however, and a rich marriage with one of the Miasnikofs, the daughter of a ferryman who had made his fortune in the mines of the Oural, consoles him for his disgrace. One of his daughters marries Prince Bielossielski, whose picture-gallery, known as "the cupboard," so greatly amused Madame Vigée-Lebrun. Another became the Countess of Laval; her salon at St. Petersburg was much frequented by the French refugees.

The Countess Braniçki has for neighbour, in the palace, Count Nicholas Saltykof, who is equally pro-vided for at the Empress's expense, on the footing of an Imperial Highness: two hundred thousand roubles a year! Officially he is merely the guardian of the Grand-Dukes Alexander and Constantine, but he is really a confidential agent of Catherine in all her affairs with Paul, whose downfall he endeavours to bring about. In spite of all this, Paul himself, later on makes him Field-marshal and Grand Master of the Order of Malta.

Ribeaupierre, whom we have seen in connection with Mamonof, is a sort of confidant of the favourite. He is a Swiss, belonging to a family said to be of Alsatian origin, settled in Switzerland since the time of the Revocation of Nantes. Coming to St. Petersburg in 1782 with a commission from Grimm, some cameos bought for Lanskoï, he is received by the Empress as subordinate to Betzki in her reading of the French classics. Of good appearance, and blithe humour, he has the further advantage of lending himself to an easy pun, "Ris, beau Pierre," and Catherine, as we know, is far from disliking this kind of fun. He has also a son, whom the Empress takes a fancy to, and whom she keeps by her in the palace. When the second Turkish war breaks out, he follows the example of those who are aiming at a brilliant career under the great Empress, and we find him brigadier under the walls of Ismaïl. A Turkish ball cuts short his ambitious dreams. But, with a son brought up almost on the knees of Catherine, he leaves a family of which Russia becomes the adopted country. The *protégé* of the sovereign left some memoirs, which do credit to his teacher.

We should not forget the Baron von Asseburg, also the writer of memoirs to which we have frequently turned : his specialty is in marriages ; he is a sort of commercial traveller in this species, always on the search through the little German courts, receiving four thousand roubles a year for his trouble and travelling expenses, and carrying on a correspondence in cryptogram, in which the proposed marriages are alluded to as "works for publication," and the Empress as "the publisher."

We know hardly anything of the part played by Rogerson, Catherine's English physician, apart from his professional duties, though there is little doubt that it was a considerable one. In 1786 the Comte de Ségur, announcing the doctor's departure for England for six months, adds : " As he dabbles in politics as much as in medicine, and it is through his hands that the bribes are supposed to pass, I cannot but be very pleased at his absence."

After these, but still with a considerable share in the sovereign's confidence, come the staff of dependents : *valets de chambre*, tutors of natural children, and *femmes de chambre*, consulted at the critical moments which occur in the history of favouritism. Their functions are often vague and variable enough : the lackey Shkurin becomes chamberlain ; Zotof, who succeeds him, uses a liberty of speech with the sovereign which is rather those of a surly friend than a valet ; the faithful Pierekussihina is a *femme de chambre* quite unique of her kind, and is treated almost like an elder sister. Catherine, like Patiomkin, has her court and her lower court, the one as well-stocked and as bustling as the other, and the two so frequently overlapping as to become indistinguishable.

CHAPTER IV.

THE COURT OF CATHERINE.

I.

" Louis XIV. would have been jealous of his sister Catherine, or he would have married her, so as to have at all events a fine levee," wrote the Prince de Ligne in 1787. The courtiers and correspondents of Catherine were good, very good, at hyperbole. But this time the admiring enthusiasm of the amiable cosmopolitan is in perfect harmony with the universal opinion of the contemporary world, all uniting in praise of the luxury, the magnificence, the incomparable splendour, of the new Versailles on the misty shores of the Neva. Is this to admit that his way of appreciating, by comparison, the merits of a court to which he at one time contributed some of his charm, can be accepted at all points ? Certainly not. The voice of the people may sometimes be the voice of God ; it is not always that of the historian. In the present case we could not accept its echo without certain serious reservations.

The *Roi-Soleil*, in his Versailles, entered upon the heritage of Francis I. and Catherine de Medicis; it was

quite another thing to enter upon the heritage of Peter
the Great at Tsarskoïe-Sielo. When he came to take
up his new abode, Louis XIV. came from Saint-Germain
and Fontainebleau, without counting the Louvre. The
Saint-Germain, the Fontainebleau, the Louvre of Catherine, was that little wooden house, like a showman's
booth, which people still flock to see at St. Petersburg,
in which the great Tsar had lived. The contrast was
enormous. It is enough for the glory of the modern
Semiramis to have in some measure filled up the gap.
My purpose in the following pages is to indicate just
what that measure was, and it is from this point of
view that the rapid sketch to which I must confine
myself finds its natural connection with the general
purport of this study, by offering a certain serious
historical interest. With its lights and shadows, its
varnish of Western culture and its inner depths of
Asiatic barbarism, its requirements and its vulgarities,
the real aspect of the court of Catherine gives a partial,
but still a faithful, and an amusing, picture of the great
work of transformation from which the Russia of to-day
has sprung.

Before Peter I., the Muscovite sovereigns have their
courtiers, but, properly speaking, no court. The "assem-
blies" at the imperial palace are also the work of the
great Tsar. But in order to induce the Muscovite lords
to attend them, he had to threaten corporal punishment.
Even under Elizabeth the imperial theatre is filled on
gala days by ukase. To Catherine II. belongs the
honour of having inaugurated a new *régime* of absolute
liberty in this respect, under which the Count de Ségur

can escape from the charms of the imperial *lotto*, and
even excuse himself in some caustic lines, over which
the sovereign is the first to laugh. The court of Elizabeth had greatly disappointed d'Éon, what was really
fine in the Empress's retinue seeming to him to be
confined to ten persons at the outside ; "the rest is
anyhow, and, so long as the wardrobe is garnished with
some kind of stuff, with some sort of gold or silver
trimming, no one minds if the coat is of grey cloth and
the trimmings of green velvet . . . The receptions are
fine, but monotonous. There is a certain ceremony, but
hardly any society." Society, in fact, had scarcely had
time to disengage itself from the confusion of ranks, or
their levelling under the still brutal weight of an Eastern
despotism. The gentlemen of the court were scarcely
distinguishable from the servants who waited upon
them. On leaving service these people, lackeys, heiducs,
cooks, pastry-cooks, took rank in the military hierarchy
of the empire, becoming ensigns or under-lieutenants,
and ended their days as burgomaster in some provincial
town. In spite of this, Catherine was forced to issue
orders forbidding the persons of her retinue to strike or
beat the servants, as they had been accustomed to do.

The receptions and *fêtes* with which the widow of
Peter III. inaugurates her reign display from the very
first a note of superior elegance, despite their definitely
Oriental colour. The pomp displayed on the occasion
of the coronation is relatively modest, and the expense
trifling, compared with what takes place at Rheims, for
instance, under similar circumstances. Prince Trubetzkoï is entrusted with the organization of the cere-

mony, and receives fifty thousand roubles (two hundred and fifty thousand francs) for general expenses, a pound of gold and ten pounds of silver for the crown, four ermine skins for the imperial mantle. The amount does not prove sufficient, it is true, as usually happens under all latitudes. For eight days there is search for the golden ball which is supposed to be contained in the imperial treasure: it has disappeared, and a fresh expense is incurred. The disorder at the court is so great that at the moment of Her Majesty's departure for Moscow, where the coronation is to take place, her servants are on the point of going on strike: they have not had food for three days! The sovereign does not take with her a very numerous retinue, twenty-eight persons in all, but they demand for their transport no less than sixty-three equipages, with three hundred and ninety-five horses. The Tsarevitch travels separately, with a train of twenty-seven equipages, drawn by two hundred and fifty-seven horses. These equipages are literally houses on wheels. A hundred and twenty oak barrels, hooped with iron, carry six hundred thousand pieces of silver money for Her Majesty's personal expenses, for giving away to the people, to the poor, etc.

The ceremony takes place September 23, 1762. Catherine herself places the diadem on her own head, after which she goes to the altar, alone, and administers the sacrament to herself. The following days are taken up with the interminable series of deputations. Kissing the hand is not enough for the expression of their homage, they still bow to the ground, a practice which Catherine later on prides herself on having suppressed. One after another goes by, grovelling in turn in the dust before the throne: the representatives of the Russian nobility, and of the knights of the Baltic provinces, the officers of the Guard, the deputies from the Asiatic nations, the Greeks, the Armenians, the Calmucks, the Cossacks of Iaïk and of the Volga, and, in their midst, the scholars from the seminary of La Troïtza, dressed in white dresses, embroidered with gold, and crowned with green leaves. This procession once over, the court *fêtes*, balls, masquerades, gala dinners, plays, alternate with popular rejoicings. At the imperial theatre a performance of *Zaïre* in French follows a Russian tragedy. The maids of honour take part in a ballet, and the orchestra is composed of gentlemen of the court. But a *cortège* representing "the triumph of Minerva" receives a somewhat cold welcome on its way through the streets. No one of that name had ever been heard of. And no one knows what she is supposed to triumph over: is it over the *matushka* who has just assumed the crown for the greater welfare of her people? Besides, a recent ukase has ordered decent vestments to be worn in the streets, and forbidden the wearing of disguise. Why are these people in extravagant costumes not arrested? A people's theatre, with marionnettes and German conjuring tricks, has still less success. It is supposed to be indebted to the aid of the devil. A Frenchman named Dumoulin had, the year before, sent everybody flying with the exhibition of "a movable head," which had caused the deepest terror.

Catherine herself comes to be somewhat alarmed at the luxurious fashions which these novel travesties bring

about. A ukase is issued, forbidding the importation
of lace and stuffs of silk and silver. The Baron de
Breteuil takes it very coolly in his dispatch of January
9, 1763 : "People may now wear neither gold nor silver
. . . but all the same they will have to turn to our
fashions and our manufactures for things much more
simple and not less costly."

The *fêtes* continue during the whole time of Catherine's
residence at Moscow, from September 1762 to June
1763. Meanwhile, the residences in and near St.
Petersburg are put on a new footing of elegance and
comfort. The wooden palace of Elizabeth is trans-
ported to Krasnoïe-Sielo, and the new palace built in
brick by Catherine's predecessor is luxuriously fitted
up. In 1765, when Casanova visits the garden connected with the imperial residence, he still sees some
things which provoke his surprise and sarcasm : statues
blocked out by soldiers of the Guard, hump-backed
Apollos, sickly Venuses, a Sappho with the features of
an elderly gentleman with a beard, and Philemon and
Baucis represented by two young people exchanging
innocent kisses. That is a legacy of Elizabeth. But,
less than twenty years later, Longpré, the inspector
of police, is greatly overcome by the magnificence of
Tsarskoïe. There is, however, more show than taste
in the somewhat monotonous profusion of gilding and
other decorations which he enumerates with enthusiasm :
"It is impossible to see anything more *recherché* and
more sumptuous than the dressing-room, bedroom,
work-room, and boudoir of Her Majesty. The dressing-
room is all mirrors, with superb gilt frames. The bed-

room is surrounded with little colonnades from top to
bottom, covered with solid silver, half natural colour,
and half lilac. Behind the colonnades there are mirrors,
and the ceilings are painted. The work-room is surrounded in the same manner with little colonnades
covered with solid silver, half gold-colour and half blue.
Behind these colonnades there are mirrors, and the ceiling is painted. The boudoir is similarly surrounded
with little colonnades also covered with solid silver, half
natural colour and half pink. Behind these colonnades
and on the ceiling it is half mirrors and half pink.
These last three rooms are superbly decorated with
bronzes and gilt wreaths on all the colonnades." Harris
observes, for his part, that among the portraits of
crowned heads, ornamenting the walls of a country-
house which the Empress modestly and familiarly calls
her frog-pond (doubtless on account of the marshy land
around, and the Finnish name, *kireriko*, by which the
château of Tchesmé is known), there is not a single
picture in which there is design, colour, or composition,
with the single exception of a picture of West, representing the two English princes. But Wedgwood
supplied the "Frog-pond" with a wonderful service, in
which a charming batrachian in green is seen surmount-
ing some delightful English country-houses. But the
"Samson," an artificial water at Peterhof, is reported
to be the finest in Europe after that of Cassel, on the
authority, at all events, of the Abbé de Lubersac, who
assigns only the fourth place to that of Saint-Cloud,
after that of M. Bergaret, receiver-general of finances
at Nointel.

Everywhere there is the same mixture of wealth and poverty, except perhaps at the Hermitage, where Catherine does her utmost to concentrate the shining rays of her sphere, which is a very different one after all, as we have seen, and as she doubtless saw herself, from that of the *Roi-Soleil.* Count Hordt gives in his memoirs an attractive account of this annex of the big palace, built after the designs of Rastrelli in the rococo style of the time : " It comprises a whole wing of the imperial palace, and consists in a picture gallery, two great rooms where play goes on, and another with two tables for little dinners, and, by the side of these rooms, there is a covered winter garden, well lighted. You can walk about there among the trees and a prodigious quantity of flower-pots. You see and hear birds of all kinds singing, principally canaries. It is warmed by underground furnaces, and, despite the rigour of the climate, it always preserved the most even temperature. And, agreeable as all this is in itself, it is still more so on account of the liberty that reigns there. There is no sort of stiffness, the Empress has banished all etiquette. You walk about, you play cards, you sing, every one according to his fancy." The picture gallery abounds in masterpieces of the first order ; the main part of it coming from three considerable collections : that of the Baron de Thiers, lieutenant-general under Louis XV., that of Count Henri de Brühl, minister of King Augustus of Saxony, and the marvellous series of pictures collected at Houghton Hall by Robert Walpole. Among the English acquisitions there are six Salvator Rosas, among them the *Prodigal Son*, his finest picture,

the *Conception* and the *Nativity* of Murillo, the superb
compositions of Rubens for the solemn entry of the
child-cardinal at Antwerp, the *Virgin with Partridges*
of Van Dyck, for which Walpole had given £1400, and
the *Dispute of the Fathers of the Church* by Guido
Reni, which Innocent XIII. would not at first allow to
be removed out of his dominions. The Thiers collection contains two famous pictures of Raphael, the *Holy
Family, with the beardless Joseph,* and the *St. George
on Horseback.* In 1772, at the sale of the Duc de
Choiseul-Stainville, Catherine acquires the *Benedicite*
of Rembrandt, the *Doctor* of Gerard Dow (which costs
19,153 livres), the *Stag Hunt* of Wouverman (which
costs 20,700 livres), and two *Village Fêtes* of Poussin,
which belonged to the famous Comtesse Jeanne de
Verdrac, and which had cost her 37,000 livres. Then
there are the collections of Randon de Boisse, of the
Prince de Conti, of Dezallier d'Argenville, of Gostkowski,
of Tronchin, which she purchases in whole or in part ;
and the pictures painted to order by Raphael Mengs,
Angelica Kauffmann, and Sir Joshua Reynolds. In
1784 a theatre is added to the charms of the Hermitage.
" Laid out in a single vast semi-circular amphitheatre,
rising in tiers from the orchestra to the vestibule," it
unites, according to a competent authority of the time,
Armand Domergue, the stage-manager of the imperial
theatre at Moscow, "the utmost possible combination
of pomp and splendour." And the best actors and
actresses of the day, Aufresne, Floridor, Delpit, Bour-
dais, Madame Lesage, Mademoiselle Huss, act the
masterpieces of Molière and Regnard ; the divine

Païsiello conducts the orchestra, for which he composes some of his best operas, *La Serva Padrona*, *Il Matrimonio Inaspettato*, and the *Barbiere di Seviglia*, which Rossini does over again forty years later. Cimarosa, who succeeds Païsiello, writes, during his three years' residence, five hundred compositions for the court orchestra and the private orchestras of the principal members of the aristocracy. Sarti follows suit ; and, indifferent as she is to the charms of music, Catherine submits to all the exacting demands of the artistes whom the composers insist on having ; she even endures their caprices and impertinences. La Gabrielli, who has a salary of seven thousand roubles, refuses to sing to Her Majesty in private, because, she declares, Her Majesty understands nothing about it, and when the Empress points out to her that her marshals are not so well paid as she is, she makes her famous reply : " Let her make her marshals sing, then ! " The quarrels of the tenor Marchesi with another *prima donna*, la Todi, assume, under the indulgent eyes of the Tsarina, quite the importance of an affair of state.

The display becomes more and more lavish. In 1778, at a *fête* given on the occasion of the birth of Paul's eldest son, the guests play *macao* at three tables, at each of which the player who puts down a nine is entitled to a diamond, which he takes with a golden spoon out of a box-full placed at the end of the table. The game goes on for an hour and a half, after which, as the boxes are only half emptied, the players take their share of the contents. This time Harris himself is dazzled, Asiatic as all this seems to him, this realization of the fabled splendours of Golconda. The invitations to this *fête* are sent out in the name of M. Francisque Azor, an Asiatic or African proprietor of a diamond mine, a pseudonym under which one easily recognizes the squanderer of precious stones and Cashmere shawls whom we have already seen in Moldavia. This time the diamonds are not worth more than fifty roubles apiece, according to the English diplomatist's valuation ; but he speaks also of a dessert served at supper on plate which he values at two millions sterling.

The influence of the Prince of Taurida counts for much in the increase of that prodigal pomp which we find even outside the court and the circles in immediate contact with it. Igelstroem, appointed ambassador in Sweden at the end of the Swedish war, and in the very middle of the ruinous Turkish war, receives twenty thousand roubles for his salary, four thousand five hundred roubles a month for his maintenance, without including an immense amount of plate; and he is not content with that. He requires two state coaches, with six horses each, eight household officers, two runners, two chasseurs, two heiducs, two hussars to follow his coach, four horsemen, a secretary, three under-secretaries, four or six aides-de-camp, four couriers, a host of valets, a house "finer than any in Stockholm," and fifteen thousand roubles' worth of jewellery for his own person. The uniform of the gentlemen-guards who accompany the Empress outside the palace on solemn occasions, and who serve usually inside the palace, is of the utmost splendour : " blue cloth with red facings, covered with a kind of silver cuirass on which the imperial eagle is

embossed.   Arms and legs are also covered, at intervals,
by plates of silver, linked together by chains of the
same metal, which makes them look somewhat like the
arm-plates and thigh-plates of the old knights."   " The
likeness," adds the Marquis de Beausset, who gives us
these details in a dispatch of June 10, 1766, to the
Duc de Choiseul, " becomes still more striking in the
silver helmet topped with black plumes.   The top-boots
are also armed at the knee and along the side with
blades of silver."

It should be noted, however, that, according to a document dated 1767, the annual expenses of the court are
not in excess of one million one hundred thousand
roubles ; to wit :

	ROUBLES.
For the Empress's household, the salary of those who belong to it, meals, music, the play, the *menus plaisirs*, lights, hunting, and its equipment ...	900,000
The stables	100,000
The wardrobe, jewellery, and presents	100,000
	1,100,000

These figures were more than doubled, surely, during
the latter half of Catherine's reign ; compared with
those we see in the accounts of Versailles at the same
period, they are surprisingly moderate.   Louis XVI.'s
stables alone cost as much or more : 7,717,058 livres in
1786.   From 1744 to 1788, the complete household
budget of the King of France, and those of his family,
varies from thirty-two to thirty-six millions a year; or
seven times as much as that of Catherine the Great.

Much of this depends upon the great difference in
the number of persons whose expenses are reckoned up

in these accounts. Catherine is content with but few about her : twelve chamberlains, twelve ladies and gentlemen-in-waiting constitute the main part of it. We are far indeed from the four thousand persons who make up the royal household in France, without counting the military part of it, which is twice as much. The household of Catherine being thus limited, the honour of a place in it is all the more sought after. Count Mussin-Pushkin, afterwards field-marshal, is already general-in-chief when, in 1775, he receives the golden key, and he is enchanted with the promotion. All those holding these envied official positions carry out their duties with extreme exactitude and zeal. Freiline Bibikof, who is specially authorized to live outside the palace in order to look after her mother, does not fail to appear at the proper time even on the day of the great flood in 1777 : she gets to the palace by boat. Catherine treats her maids-of-honour almost as if they were her own daughters. She notices that Freiline Potocka, who has lately come to the court, has no pearls ; and she immediately seizes the opportunity of a fancy dress ball to which the girl comes in the disguise of a milkmaid, in order to slip a superb necklace into the pail that she has put down while dancing. " It is you, Madame . . . it is Your Majesty . . . " she stammers, on discovering the present. " No, the milk has curdled." But the pranks and failings of the young troop are severely punished. In 1784 a caricature goes the round of the court, in which Prince Patiomkin is represented lying on a couch, and surrounded by his three nieces, the Countesses Braniçki, Jussupof, and Skavronski, very

scantily attired, and all apparently disputing possession. Two *freilines*, Mademoiselles Buturlin and Elmpt,
both eighteen years of age, are accused of being
responsible for the drawing; they are found guilty, and
flogged until the blood is drawn, in the presence of
their companions, and then sent back to their homes.
Their disgrace, however, is not a final one. Mademoiselle Elmpt, then Madame Turshinof, re-appears at the
court a few years after, and contributes to the success
of her husband, who is appointed overseer of imperial
works. The other, the fair, witty, audacious, and dis-
sipated Countess Divof, afterwards so notorious, we have
already seen in her salon, so largely frequented by the
French refugees.

As a matter of fact, the surroundings in which the
Semiramis of the North awes and amazes all Europe
are really quite modest. As in the preceding reigns,
extreme luxury is seen side by side with poverty, and
profusion alternates with a singular parsimony. In
1791, at a masked ball given at Peterhof, the principal
staircase is not lighted. In 1792, it occurs to some one
that the pages are in want of a fresh livery; their
present livery has been in use for thirty-four years!

II.

In regard to etiquette, good manners, and even
decency, the court is equally far from its Western
models. According to a German traveller, Count
Sternberg, who visited Russia in 1792 and 1793, the

reception-room of the palace was always in a state of
the utmost disorder up to the moment of the Empress's
appearance, and the moment after her departure. A
deafening clamour, in which all the languages of Europe
and Asia are heard at once, reigns there continually.
On ball days it is worse. On these days every one
bearing any sort of military title has right of access :
now, Her Majesty's coachman has the title of lieutenant-
colonel! On ordinary reception-days it is enough to
have a sword by one's side to be able to make one's
way as far as the door of the throne-room, which is
guarded by two of the gentlemen-guards in full uniform :
silver cuirass, three-cornered hats, and arms grounded.
There is no apparent supervision, either at the door, or
on the staircase, or in the first reception-room ; no one
asks who you are or where you are going. At the time
of the Revolution, there are rumours that an attempt
at assassination is to be made by some French demagogues, and Passek, the aide-de-camp on duty, places
two warders in the vestibule of the palace ; the Empress
hears of it, and countermands the order. Entrance
into the throne-room is only permitted to those whose
names are enrolled on a list in the keeping of the two
gentlemen-guards ; but the list is a long one. Even
the Empress's dressing-room, where she gives her
private audiences, often gets crowded ; the secretaries
of state have their *entrées* every day, the procurator-
general on Sundays. A mere *valet de chambre* in
French costume stands at the door. Apart from the
liveries of the lackeys and pages, there is no special court
dress during the earlier years of the reign. In 1783, a

dress is appointed for the gentlemen, in the colours of
their respective provinces. At the same time, in order to
repress the extravagance of toilet to which the invasion
of French fashions gives more and more ruinous pro-
portions, Catherine insists on a certain uniformity of
costume among the ladies admitted to these receptions.
She adopts, first at the Hermitage and then at all the
royal residences, a Russian costume, or what is at all
events called so, in purple velvet, a costume which
would have driven Marie-Antoinette crazy. The belles
of St. Petersburg are in the utmost distress at not being
able to appear at the palace in the charming creations
of Mademoiselle Bertin, but they have to accept their
fate. They have to give up even the coiffures *à la
Reine* and *à la Belle-Poule*, for an imperial ukase forbids
any structure on the head higher than a quarter of a
Russian ell. The Grand-Duchess, Maria Feodorovna, is
in tears for a week, for she has to sacrifice some of her
magnificent hair in order to obey the common law.

Catherine, by these means, endeavours to turn back a
current already in force, and whose volume she has herself swelled. The imitation of foreign models, French
especially, has been general for the last half-century,
and it is the court which, from Peter the Great onward,
has set the example. The park at Peterhof is an imitation, on a smaller scale, of that at Versailles. Society
merely follows, as it invariably does, the example of
those above it. In 1779, a paper nominally concerned
with fashions does injustice to its title by only inserting
literary articles ; but in 1791 the *Magasin des Modes
françaises, anglaises et allemandes,* though it occasion-

ally dabbles in politics, laughing at the National Assembly and parodying the *Ça ira*, gives the most detailed information in regard to the fashions of the day in the various European capitals, Paris principally, the bonnets *à la Bergère*, and the masterpieces of Madame Treilhard, the milliner of the Palais-Royal. The tide of imitation associates itself at this moment with the anti-revolutionary movement, of which Catherine has just given the signal: the Revolution is condemned by the more extensive adoption of the forms and refinements of old French society.

The imitation, it is true, is always imperfect, often awkward to absurdity. The engravings in the *Magasin des Modes* are grotesque. The court ladies imagine that they will look like Marie-Antoinette by putting on lawn over brocade, and that they will be dressed *à la Madame Marlborough* by sewing black fringes over the first dress that comes to hand. The canal of Peterhof, which professes to rival that of Versailles, is merely a ditch a few feet wide, where nothing but children's boats could float easily. "In Russia," writes the Comte de Damas, "everything is more like a fine sketch than a finished work. The establishments are just beginning, the houses are just putting up a front, the people in charge of things do not know their own duties. . . . Dress, Asiatic among the people, French at the court, does not seem to have been quite put into order. . . . The temper of the people is muzzled rather than softened. . . . One often meets with intelligent, rarely with amiable people. . . . There are Ninettes at court, to any extent, who would find themselves quite at home again in their native villages, shaven chins that have already found out that beards were warmer, and merchants who like dealing in furs more than dealing in trinkets and fashions."

Instincts, however, remained savage, tastes were still gross. The tone of the *ancien régime* of France could scarcely be expected to prevail in a court where Peter III. distributed blows with the flat of his sword to his favourites, and treated women, in public, with the utmost indecency. "To touch the bosom," wrote a diplomatist, "is not the greatest liberty that he takes in public with ladies of the highest distinction." The corruption of manners at Versailles is the only thing that seems completely assimilated, and even this is deformed and degraded, despoiled of its cloak of elegance and discreet coquetry, stripped and exposed shamelessly in the street. In 1795 the Italian tenor Bandini and his wife, an old courtesan known all over Paris, are the lions of the greatest ladies at St. Petersburg. Princess Kurakin boasts of having passed the evening in *tête-à-tête* with Madame Mandini, awaiting the return of the singer, who comes back to them after the performance "all in sweat, in his dressing-gown and night-cap." People wear mottoes distributed by Mandini, Madame Divoff that of *Sempre pazza*. Princess Dolgoruki is conspicuous by her fervour in crying *Bravo* the moment the tenor appears on the stage, and *Fuori* the moment he retires to the wings.

And, we must admit, the main obstacle to a more perfect, delicate, and decent adoption of Western models at the court of Catherine is due to Catherine herself. Her mind, her character, her temperament, render her equally averse, not only, as she herself admits, to the rigours of an elaborate etiquette, but even more so to the charms of an elegant and cultivated *entourage*, or even to the mere habits and manners of good company. The Comte de Ségur does indeed attract her, because he flatters her, and because the distinction and correctness of his demeanour, a sort of hot-house plant brought straight from Versailles, are a form of homage whose value she thoroughly appreciates, but Léon Naryshkin amuses her more and suits her better. State dignity bores her, official ceremonies weary her, the kissing of hands is odious to her. She is sometimes very amusing on the subject.

"I finish this letter at Plescow, where I arrived at nine o'clock in the evening, after having dined with a princess who is as salt as a ham, literally salt, and this is how I found it out. On saying good-bye to her, she was going to kiss my hand, so I put my lips to her cheek, and, as the grand equerry was leading me downstairs, I somehow felt, I don't know how, as I was talking with him, the taste of salt on my lips; I burst out laughing, and told him of it; he looked at me, and saw some white on my lips. That is how I learnt that white paint is salt." And, a few days after: "Since Plescow, Mademoiselle Engelhardt, the eldest, has charge of my eyes; this is how: before she presents the ladies to me, she arranges their flowers and feathers, with which I had some terrible encounters at Plescow." The Baron de Breteuil comes to her one day at a reception to present his compliments to her; she interrupts

him : " Have you ever seen the hounds after a hare ?
You must feel that I am very much in the same situation here." But, apart even from the pack of courtiers,
always on her heels, she is ill at ease in the midst of
those very splendours with which she has filled her
palaces, embarrassed by all the pomp for which she
does not care, bored by the works of art which she does
not understand. " I am well lodged this winter," she
writes in 1777; "all sorts of admirable things are heaped
up all around me, things which are good for nothing,
and which I never use. I am like that Khan of the
Kirghizs, to whom the Empress Elizabeth gave a house
at Oremburg, and who had a tent put up in the court to
live in. I keep in my own corner."

Her corner is the Hermitage, where, in a less gorgeous
frame, there are two distinct divisions: the *décor*
admired by Armand Domergue, and the *mise-en-scène* of
reception days, the artistic collections and the gala
representations, make up one, which is meant for the
public ; the other belongs to the sovereign, and there she
escapes from the crowd to the pleasant familiarity of the
private gatherings to which only a favoured few have
access. These gatherings are like neither Versailles
nor Trianon, nor yet the Hôtel Rambouillet, nor even
the bourgeois salon of Madame Geoffrin. It is not the
French style of wit that prevails there: the Comte de
Ségur himself sometimes forgets his courtly manners,
and Léon Naryshkin, who usually gives the tone, has
nothing in common with a gentleman of the court of
Louis XIV., not even with Saint-Simon's Roquelaure,
supposing that such a Roquelaure ever existed. He has

spilt his blood on no field of battle, he governs no province. He has, as grand equerry, the charge of the royal stables ; but, having one day found a cat installed in the arm-chair reserved for him in the office of this administration, he declares that his place has been disposed of, and never sets foot in it again. His style of wit tends mainly towards puns. One day a door creaks so loudly during a discussion in regard to the declaration of war against Turkey as to drown the voice of the speakers ; whereupon he declares "que c'est *la Porte* qui demande du secours à la Grèce." He jokes in public over his conjugal mishaps (his wife is the daughter of a mere Cossack), and parodies before the Empress a song then popular, "Voilà l'objet de ma flamme," pointing out one of his own servants who enjoys the favour of Madame Naryshkin, and singing : " Voilà l'objet de ma *femme*." When he is not making puns, he rambles on all subjects, and employs the most extravagant and sometimes the grossest buffooneries, taking lessons in the art, it is said, from the actor Renaud. Catherine finds him one day in her own work-room, sprawling on the sofa and bawling out some senseless song ; as he refuses to quit the place or be silent, she fetches her sister-in-law, and both arm themselves with a bundle of nettles, and set to beating him with them. Catherine calls him " the born harlequin," but she confesses that she is passionately fond of hearing him talk politics, and that no one has ever made her laugh so heartily. She sings his merits in two burlesque poems (*Leoniana*), which she brings on the stage in her comedy of *L'Insouciant*. Amusing herself one day at the game of epitaphs, she composes the following for her favourite companion in her hours of leisure and relaxation :

"FOR THE INFORMATION OF POSTERITY.

INSCRIPTION

*For the foundation-stone of the country-house of M. le grand
écuyer, Léon Naryshkin :*

This is the abode
Of Sir Léon Naryshkin, grand equerry.
No frisky horse hates him, for he never mounted one.
In his youth, Dame Nature promised to make him handsome :
No one knows why she did not keep her word.
When he came to marry, he married the women he liked least.
He loved wine, women, and dress, yet no one ever saw him
Drunk, in love, or well-dressed.
He shaved himself, lest the barber should cut him.
And the greater the occasion, the more numerous were the
razor-cuts
On his face.
His friends said he was very respectful at the outset,
And very ill-tempered afterwards.
He danced much, and was blithe and active at all times
Except when his stoutness of body hindered his left leg
From following his right.
He was rich, and never had a penny in his pocket.
He liked to go to the market, where he always bought what he
did not want.
What he loved best were the hundred fathoms that you see.
He planted them with new country boxes
Every year, which were reached by
Winding paths, laid out
With shrubs, bordered by
Ponds and streams
Which were dry, when
There was no rain.
Despite which, he passed the larger part of the year out of doors.
Blithe and gay was his motto ;
Cards his element ;
Laughter followed in his track."

After Naryshkin, another intimate of the Hermitage, Baron Vanjura, is distinguished by his talent for bringing his thick-set hair down to his eyebrows by wrinkling his forehead, as if it were a wig. On account of this talent he is named captain of the gay company that Catherine gathers about her. She herself is clever at moving her right ear, while the rest of her face remains motionless. Let us not blame her too severely : twenty years later another Empress, Archduchess by birth, Marie-Louise, will do much the same at the Tuileries. We should not forget, among these buffoons, the court fool Matrena Danilovna Tiepliskaïa, a woman belonging to a family of small shopkeepers settled at Iaroslav, equally vulgar in mind and manners, whom the Empress lodges in the palace, covers with diamonds, and whom she allows to call her sister. Questioning her one day why she professes such dislike of the King of Sweden, she answers : " Because he is a German, and with us, when a German comes to the house, we wash and sweep up everything after him, even the handle of the door on which he has put his hand."

Yes, this court is a Versailles with at least ten centuries less of those monarchical traditions, that high culture, which in France have blossomed out into a final burst of splendour. It is Versailles copied by a workman who lacked all the materials for his task, alike in substance and in colour ; mere scene-painting on coarse canvas. But the resemblance is there, and, if you would see it even in small details, notice in some corner of the imperial palace that gentleman-in-waiting, whose mouth seems settled into a smile of fixed irony, whose sarcastic eyes seem to pierce through all the pomp and show about him, and see the bareness of misery beneath, raising the silk and velvet that cover it, and displaying the shames that lurk below.   Presently, when he returns to his home, he will write to his friend Vorontsof a letter in which the smallest incidents of the day are sifted by a pitiless criticism, in which all the people whom he has but lately been elbowing are lashed with an inexhaustible abundance of sarcasm and invective : it is the future incendiary of Moscow, "the Russian Saint-Simon," as he has been called ; a Saint-Simon at once sharper and more jovial, bitterer and less sceptical, having no such reasons for hating the world about him as the other, who was, if the expression is not too free (he himself has set the example of all kinds of liberties !), a *raté* of genius ; on the contrary, he has had a brilliant career before him, he has had but to choose what place he would have at the side of the heir to the throne ; still, always unsatisfied, even with the prince who has had nothing but favour for him, even with the future which does but smile upon him ; a universal fault-finder, detractor, and cynic ; an imitator of Saint-Simon, yes, in this correspondence with the London exile, itself all but a masterpiece, but a precursor too, one of the first representatives of that state of soul which, fortunately for Russia, is as yet only the heritage of a small group of disciples.

A great empire may be created in a short time ; a Versailles cannot be improvised.   It is enough to have succeeded, as Catherine did, in giving so much of the appearance of majesty and grandeur to an estab-

lishment only set on foot, or at least on a European
footing, a few years back; especially as, in doing
this much, she has had to do some violence to herself. "It is curious to observe," writes the Baron de
Breteuil in 1763, "the painful care that the Empress
takes, on court-days, to please all her subjects. For me,
knowing as I do the character of this princess, and
seeing her adapt herself with such unparalleled sweetness and grace to all that, I can easily imagine how
much it must cost her, and how much she feels the
obligation of submitting to it." Her way of reigning,
like her way of ruling, has none the less a certain air of
recent military conquest. The banquets at which she
appears among her officers of the Guard, dressed in
their costume, and emptying her glass of traditional
vodka with them, recall the violent struggles out of
which her empire has arisen. Her court is always a
little like a camp. And that is why the furthest point
of the pomp and magnificence with which she strives to
reach the level of the monarchical traditions of the
West, is reached only in travelling over the roads of
Taurida.

III.

Unlike Peter I., who was an indefatigable traveller,
Catherine rarely travels. And it is not only her personal tastes, which are more or less stationary, that
keep her at home; every change of residence is a
source of terrible danger; she has no sooner left St.
Petersburg, in 1764, for the purpose of visiting Livonia

and Esthonia, than Mirovitch's plot breaks out behind her, with its warning of how frail is the structure of her fortune, and how needful it is to watch over it closely.   Later still, even when her throne is secure against any common plot, the mere presence of Paul remains a constant menace.   When she leaves the capital, she arranges that, at the smallest alarm, men on whom she has the utmost reliance are to seize the heir to the throne, and bring him to her.   However, when she does travel, it is for some length of time. The distances are great, and the Empress cannot seem to be in a hurry.   The journey in the Crimea (in the Taurida, as she wishes her conquest to be called, in memory of vaguely wonderful histories of the past) lasts six months.   There are two thousand kilometres to cover, and the road first of all has to be made. Between St. Petersburg and Moscow there are easy relays, decent enough stopping-places, and the journey is both rapid and easy.   In the Baltic provinces the castles of the Livonian and Esthonian lords offer her not only the warmest hospitality, but an unsuspected luxury and comfort.   Between St. Petersburg and Kherson, about a third of the way is a literal desert.   We know already how Patiomkin peoples this desert.

The departure takes place January 18, 1787.   The carriage of Her Majesty is drawn by thirty horses ; it contains a room in which eight persons can sit down, a card-table, a small library, and all the conveniences : it is almost the equivalent of a modern *train de luxe.* The favourite Mamonof, the inseparable Mademoiselle Protassof, and the not less inseparable Léon Naryshkin, take their places with Catherine, who moreover invites, on the first day, Count Cobenzl, the Austrian envoy, on the following day, the Comte de Ségur. There are fourteen other carriages and a hundred and twenty-four sledges for the rest of the suite. It freezes to seventeen degrees. The English envoy, Fitz-Herbert, is also among the company. The Spanish envoy, Normandez, who has vainly asked for a place, is furious with rage, according to Castéra.

On its way, the caravan finds wooden palaces, hastily set up at the sleeping-places, and, at the relays, covered galleries, with tables laid out with refreshments. The plate used on each occasion is used only once, and becomes the property of the valets. There is an immense profusion, an immense waste, great disorder too, and little comfort. "All our carriages," writes the Prince de Ligne, "are full of peaches and oranges, our valets are drunk with champagne, and I die of hunger, for everything is cold and horrid . . . Nothing is warm, except the water we drink."

In the Ukraine, Catherine is somewhat disappointed : Bezborodko, who has had charge of the material organization of the affair, and who is alarmed at the amount of money which it is wasting, has told the governor to be economical. This is no other than the illustrious Rumiantsof ; he does not require to be told twice, and he cuts down preparations to what is strictly necessary, and neglects to trick out Kief, the holy city, which the Empress has looked forward to exhibiting to her guests. "Tell the Empress that it is my business to take cities, not to paint them," he replies to Mamonof,

who has been told to make a complaint. The enchantment which has been longed for, dreamed of, expected,
by the Empress, only begins in the Crimea. There
it is Patiomkin who has arranged the *mise-en-scène*.
One of his assistants, Tchertkof, is himself scarcely able
to understand the marvels that he has contributed to
bring about : " I went with His Highness to the Taurida
. . . two months before the Empress's arrival . . . and
I asked myself what he was going to show Her Majesty.
There was nothing ! On returning with Her Majesty,
God only knows what miracles have happened, and the
devil only knows where all these buildings, armies, popu-
lations, Tartars in splendid costumes, Cossacks, ships, all
came from. I walked in a dream. I could not believe
my own eyes." This amazement is shared by all who
saw the transformation, brought about by some magic
wand in these desert steppes. " By what marvel," asks
Langeron, " can such wonders be produced ? " But
he answers the question himself. " It must be admitted,
that they were caused by tyranny and terror, and
will entail the ruin of several provinces. All the
people were turned out of certain populous districts
of Little Russia and those parts through which the
Empress was not to pass, in order to populate these
deserts ; a thousand villages were depopulated for a
time, and all their inhabitants, with all their herds,
taken to the different places marked out. They were
made to set up, hastily, pretended villages on the shores
nearest to the Dnieper, and mere façades further away.
The Empress having once passed by, the unhappy
people were sent back again ; many of them died from

the consequences of this transplantation . . . Having been governor-general of these provinces for thirty years, I have been able to find out these things for certain: they at first seemed to be fabulous." This testimony is precise, authoritative, and conclusive.

At Kief, the party embarked in order to go down the Dnieper. This kind of locomotion was quite to Catherine's taste. It is in this way that, in 1767, she had gone down the Volga as far as Kostroma, taking with her the ambassadors from Vienna, Berlin, and Copenhagen ; the French envoy was not among them, but the King's minister restrained his feelings. Ten galleys, " all covered, divided into separate rooms, and furnished ; one of them, her own, having a complete set of rooms, with a sort of salon in which," according to the Baron von Asseburg, " she dined with twelve persons without the slightest inconvenience," were at that time sufficient to carry her and her retinue. This time it was quite another affair. The flotilla comprised not less than eighty ships with three thousand men on board. A water-colour of John Lindsay, the painter of this wandering court and show, gives us a picturesque view of it at the moment of Catherine's meeting with Ponia-towski. Three great sailing ships are at the head, equal in size, and uniform in their red and gold decoration. On the bridge they have a kind of pavilion with bay windows ; above, a platform, on which soldiers are ranged in battle array. The first of these galleys (bearing the name of *Dnieper*) is that of the Empress. Side by side with her the *Boug* has on board Prince Patiom-kin and his two nieces, the Countesses Braniçki and

Skavronski. A little further back a third bark, the *Desna*, serves as dining-room. They follow the *Snow* with Counts Bezborodko, Anhalt, and Levachof; the *Seim*, with the foreign ministers, including the "diplomatic jockey," otherwise the Prince de Ligne; the *Impet* with Léon Naryshkin; the *Orel* with Count Tshernishof and his daughter; the *Joz* with a crowd of less important courtiers, private secretaries, and the like. The *Samara* and the *Kuban* are given over to the provisions and cooking. The *Tavel* and the *Don* serve as military escort. "Gold and silk," relates the Comte de Ségur, "glitter in the handsome rooms constructed on the decks. Every guest finds on board a room and dressing-room equally elegant and luxurious, a comfortable sofa, an excellent bed in coloured taffeta, and a mahogany writing-table. There is music on every galley. A swarm of little boats leads and surrounds this squadron."

Poniatowski spends three millions in three months in order to meet the Empress at Kaniof, salute her with fireworks, chat with her for three-quarters of an hour, and receive from Bezborodko the assurance that the war with Turkey is not coming off! It will cost him less, very shortly, to live side by side with the sovereign on the Quay of the Neva at St. Petersburg. Only, by that time he will have lost his crown, and deprived his country of its political existence. The fellow-travellers on this fairy voyage are scarcely aware of this royal interlude at all. The genius of the Prince of Taurida affords them every day such very different distractions! "All the stopping-places are equally marked out so as to avoid the slightest fatigue. The fleet only stops over against towns or villages picturesquely situated. Immense flocks cover the prairies, groups of peasants enliven the sea-shore, an immense crowd of youths and maidens comes out in boats, singing the rustic airs of their native lands." A near neighbour, on board the *Seim*, of the Comte de Ségur, from whom we take these details, the Prince de Ligne awakes him every morning by knocking at the thin partition which separates their beds, and reciting impromptus. An hour after, the prince's chasseur brings the young diplomatist a letter of six pages, in which " wisdom, folly, politics, gallantry, military stories, and epigrams " are all combined in an astounding mixture, and "never was anything more regularly kept up than this odd daily correspondence between an Austrian general and a French ambassador sleeping side by side on the same galley, not far from the Empress of the North, and sailing down the Borysthenes through the Cossacks' country on their way to the country of the Tartars."

With this Austrian general and this French ambassador, it is Europe, organized and cultured Europe, that Catherine thus drags behind her across the country of the Cossacks and the Tartars, and through the fantastic land of a wonder-working imagination, the final caress of an all-powerful favourite to the pride of an ambitious mistress.

A few misadventures interrupt for a moment this long enchantment. Admirably constructed and appointed from the decorative point of view, the ships of the fleet are less conspicuous for their nautical qualities. One day the Empress's ship is carried along by the current, and dashed against the side ; she is in serious danger. She forbids the incident to be mentioned, since the foreign diplomatists, left with Normandez at St. Petersburg, will do their best to exaggerate it. At Kaïdak, thirty leagues from Kherson, they all disembark ; and at Kherson they meet with Joseph, a little ashamed of having accepted a very unceremonious invitation, not allowing anything of his feeling to appear, but venting his grudge in the surly bulletins that he sends to Field-marshal Lascy, in which he defends himself from the imputation of sharing in the delight of his imperial friend and his other companions :

" The confusion which reigns is inexpressible. The disembarkation was a long and painful process. There are more things and people on the ships than there are vehicles to hold or horses to draw. One runs in one direction, and every one else follows suit. Prince Potemkin alone, crazy after music, has a hundred and twenty musicians with him, and a poor officer having burnt his hands with powder, it is four days before he can find any one to attend to him. The land part of the expedition is in a state of disorder of which no one can give an idea ; part of the carriages are still on the water ; every one takes *kibitkas*, the vehicles of the country, to carry his baggage. In these immense plains every one tries to get ahead, six, eight carriages abreast, and, despite the fact that they are going four relays a day, the carriages get broken, and one finds plate, bedding, and baggages lying all over the steppes. The food is copious, but for the most part detestable, cold, and hard. With the exception of the Empress, who is most amiable, and of some gentlemen whose society is very tolerable, the strangers especially, it would be a regular penance."

We may pardon the august traveller for his strictures on Catherine's *cuisine:* the very day of his meeting with the sovereign, he nearly had to go without any dinner at all, the members of the commissary department having lost their way or been upset with a *kibitka.* Prince Patiomkin, after his usual manner, saves the situation, by turning cook, in company with Count Branicki. Between them they manufacture a dinner, which indeed the principal guest finds detestable. His bad humour lasts all through the voyage. At one time he thinks it ridiculous to have crossed impracticable ways in order to see "a couple of Angora goats in a sort of English garden," improvised by Patiomkin in the neighbourhood of Baktchissaraï. At another time it strikes him that a company of bombardiers has been brought all the way from St. Petersburg, a distance of two thousand versts, in order to set off some fireworks at Karassubasar.

Catherine, for her part, does not or will not see anything of all that. She enjoys unreservedly all the marvellous spectacles unrolled before her eyes. She is persuaded that the Crimea will one day pay with usury all the expense that she has had in conquering and visiting it. Only on the way back do we find her enthusiasm a little checked. She has had reports telling of bad harvests. A famine seems imminent, and she does not see how it is to be faced. The sum of four millions of roubles assigned for travelling expenses is not half enough. But Europe has been dazzled, and one must pay for all that glory and advantage. Russia will pay, as it always does.

Poor Russia is far from being dazzled, and it could scarcely be so. It has not been invited, it has seen nothing. Bolotof relates that at Toula, where the sovereign's arrival was announced for midday, the streets were crowded from sunrise. But scarcely is Her Majesty's carriage signalled than the whole crowd prostrates itself in the dust, and remains so during the whole defile of the imperial *cortége*. When a few heads dare to lift themselves, the Empress is already at a distance.

The new splendours enveloping its present monarchs, in their European costume, are not made for a nation still under the bonds of Tartar conquest. To obey, and to worship, remains its lot, without the least share in the pleasures bought by its blood and sweat, without understanding them, without even seeing them.

CHAPTER V.

I.

THE Turkish war, with its part successes, part defeats; the Swedish war, still less fortunate, following after the journey in the Crimea, mark a decline. In 1792 the great scenic artist of these wonderful transformations dies on a Moldavian road by the side of a ditch; that marks the end of an epoch. Catherine is now left alone to bear the weight of the increasing burden with which thirty years of almost invariably successful efforts have weighted her shoulders, the colossal edifice of her fortune together with that of the immense empire whose bounds she has extended; alone with Zubof! And Génet, the revolutionary diplomatist whom she still tolerates at her court, writes to Dumouriez: "Such unbounded confidence in so little capable a man seems to show that the Empress, disliking the power which Prince Potemkin had arrogated to himself, wishes to show now that she is the sole mistress. But pitiless nature is against this last effort of her *amour-propre*. Catherine II. is visibly on the decline, and melancholy begins to take possession of her soul."

We see it in her private correspondence, this melancholy coming down slowly, like a cold and dark fog about her, once so radiant with youth and vigour. Her moral and her physical health give way at once. Even on the serene countenance that she always shows in public, Génet observes " certain signs betokening dropsy." She struggles bravely ; she boasts one day that she has walked two or three versts, between the Winter Palace and the Hermitage, to prove that she is still active and nimble. She doses herself too, after her fashion, with quack medicines : " I fancy it is gout in my stomach," she writes to one of her intimate friends ; " I am trying to drive it out with pepper and a glass of Malaga that I drink every day."

But her empire too shows, to the careful observer, alarming signs of weakness and distress. In a letter to Count Vorontsof, dated April 3, 1793, Bezborodko draws up a report on the general situation, and it presents a very dark picture : against the twenty-five ships that the Porte can put in line in the Black Sea, there are only nine, and these half rotten, on account of the bad quality of the wood used in their construction ; the fleet of oared galleys on which so much reliance is placed, no longer exists : Mordvinof, who has had charge of it, has only thought of filling his pockets. Patiomkin, who at least knows his men, has never thought much of him, but the new favourite takes him under his protection, as he does Ribas, who is worth no more ; the land forces are in better condition, but they cost a great deal of money, ill-managed as they are, and there is not enough to keep them in working order ; nine millions are owing for the maintenance of the fleet, and they are nowhere to be found ; the court runs away with three million roubles a year, and makes two millions of debts ; the maintenance of the Countess Braniçki alone costs two hundred thousand roubles, and that of Count Nicholas Saltykof as much ; the commerce of the country might bring in a large revenue if it were not under the control of a half-mad poet, Dierjavin, who is bringing it to the verge of ruin.

Bezborodko is a grumbler, but his testimony is not the only one. It is the almost unanimous opinion that a terrible crisis is at hand ; that Catherine's policy has strained all the springs of the machine of government beyond their furthest point of resistance ; that the supply, on all sides, is unequal to the demand, and that Russia must give way under the burdens that have been laid upon it. Catherine remains almost alone in her invariable optimism, and, if she does for an instant descry the heaped clouds darkening the horizon, not without a momentary shiver, she puts it down rather to a defect in her sight than to a change in things themselves : age, she says, makes one look at the dark side of things. And she immediately seeks to react against this impression, which, in her eyes, is a mere weakness. She will be gay ; and "I am gay," she writes to Grimm, February 15, 1796, "gay as a lark." She refuses to consider herself ill. "Up to the present I am in excellent health," she declares at that time. She plans new diversions. She sets on foot an expedition for seizing Count Stroganof by main force, and bringing him back to the court : he is himself in ill-health, and shuts himself up in a country-house near St. Petersburg, which she bombards with cannon-shots. And when the time comes for her to take a prominent place in this anti-revolutionary coalition, the manner in which she announces to Grimm that Suvorof is *en route* is as blithe as that in which she started the first campaign against the Turks: "They say that 60,000 Russians have set out for the shores of the Elbe, to put an end to the disasters in Germany; they say that Marshal Suvorof is at their head; they say lots of other things, and we shall see lots more yet; it is the magic-lantern in which we shall see what we shall see. Good-bye, 'fag'; look out for the claws."

And now it is herself who, ere the first of her soldiers has crossed the frontier, feels the claws of adverse fortune catching her full in the heart, for the first time, and leaving her overwhelmed by this unforeseen, disastrous, deadly blow. The joyous trumpet-note of war, which she sends echoing in the ears of her "fag," is on the 13th of August 1796; next day is a joyous day for her: the Count von Haga and the Count von Wasa (Gustavus, the future King of Sweden, and his uncle, the Duke of Sudermania, Regent during the prince's minority) arrive at St. Petersburg. They come officially for the purpose of declaring the adhesion of Sweden to the coalition formed against Republican France, but their visit has really quite another aim. For a long time Catherine has dreamt of a marriage between the Crown Prince of Sweden and her grand-daughter Alexandrine, the eldest daughter of Paul. The princess has been brought up with this idea. One day as she was sitting on the Empress's knees, the sovereign opened before her a portfolio filled with portraits, asking her which prince she would like to marry, and the child, without hesitation, pointed to the portrait of Gustavus. The moment is now come to realize this ten years' dream. The young people are now aged, respectively, fourteen and seventeen. But difficulties have arisen. The Regent fancies he sees the hand of Catherine in the plot of Armfeldt against his throne, and he has avenged himself by turning the foreign policy of his country into a direction absolutely contrary to the Empress's wishes, while at the same time he plans a marriage between his nephew and the daughter of the Duke of Mecklenberg-Schwerin. The betrothal has been celebrated in November 1795, and he has sent the Count von Schwerin to St. Petersburg in order to notify the fact, while negotiations are set on foot at Stockholm with M. Le Hoc, the envoy of the French Republic. But Catherine refuses to see the Count von Schwerin, and seems on the point of breaking the Mecklenberg alliance with cannon-shots. The Duke of Sudermania bends before the storm ; a secret agent of the French refugees, Christian the Genevese, formerly secretary of Calonne, has succeeded in gaining him over to more conciliatory and favourable views in regard to the anti-revolutionary alliance. With the aid of Mademoiselle Huss, the French actress, who is the mistress of Markof, the confidential friend of the new favourite, he succeeds in winning over Zubof himself, to the point at all events of a compromise, satisfactory to both parties. The Baron Budberg, a wary diplo-

matist, who has already served in Germany in regard
to matrimonial negotiations, is sent from St. Petersburg
to Stockholm on a semi-official mission.   Soon after
Le Hoc receives his *congé*, and the Regent, whom
Catherine has been abusing as a "scoundrel," writes to
her to assure her that the marriage with the Princess
of Mecklenberg shall never come off while he is in
power, and that the French alliance is abandoned.   The
Empress has insisted on the formal rupture of the
betrothal celebrated in November, and the visit of the
prince and his nephew to St. Petersburg to ask for the
hand of Alexandra Pavlovna, and, before the threat of
military operations with which this demand is accompanied, the Duke of Sudermania has half pledged
himself : he has given his formal promise that the
betrothal to which she so greatly objects shall never
be followed up, and he consents to come to St. Petersburg, without, however, making any engagement, as he
does not feel justified in setting aside the obstacle of
difference of religion which exists in regard to the union
desired by Catherine.   Catherine is once more annoyed ;
she declares that if the Regent and his ministers continue to talk of obstacles that have no common-sense,
" they are utterly God-forsaken " ; but she is obliged at
last to give in.   The two princes once in her capital,
and at hand, she will soon find means to arrange things.

They arrive, and for two weeks there seems small
chance of ever coming to an agreement.   The Duke of
Sudermania is still as reserved as ever ; and neither
Zubof, nor Markof, nor Catherine can see the way to get
him out of it.   Now, the sovereign will not give way an

inch: no marriage, no alliance ; the altar or the battle-field. But suddenly the unexpected happens : on September 4, after a dinner at court, as they are going down to the garden to take coffee, Gustavus approaches the Empress, and, without further preamble, declares, with all the ingenuous ardour of his seventeen years, that he is in love with the Princess Alexandrine, and that he asks her hand in marriage.

What has happened ? An idyll has suddenly come to flower on this dunghill of dubious intrigues and under-hand manœuvres. Two young people have met under the warm sun of August, and, across the mumbling voices of prosing politicians, their hearts have spoken the eternal language of youth and love. From the first day that they have met the all-powerful charm has done its work. On the day before, the princess had lost a dog that she was deeply attached to, and had cried all day. Madame de Lieven is distressed at the thought of her being seen with red eyes. Ah, how quickly those tears are dried under the sun of the summer now drawing to an end ! So burning, indeed, is that sun, so prodigal of its last rays, that the devoted governess is quite concerned for a moment when she sees the young couple unconsciously leave the protecting shade of the trees, and go on their way under the full blaze of light. But Catherine sees the movement she makes to recall the rash young people, and stops her with a smile. And the romance goes on its swift and flitting course : she is fourteen, he seven-teen ! After the walks, the dance. On August 28 there is a ball at the Grand-Duke's palace, and next day the Grand-Duchess feels bound to report to the Empress what has happened. This time it is not the wife of the heir to the throne, it is a mother who writes: "My dearest mother, I feel it my duty to tell Your Imperial Majesty of what happened last night; it seemed to me to augur well, for the attentions of the King to Alexandrine were very marked. He scarcely danced with any one else; even when it was past midnight, seeing that the child was asking me if she might have another dance, he went up to the Regent, and said something in his ear, at which the Regent began to laugh heartily. I asked him what it was, and he said: 'What he asked me was, whether the young princesses would be allowed to dance again. Having told him yes, he said: Oh, then I must have another dance too!' And he danced again with Alexandrine."

Four days after, it is Catherine herself who, after another ball, given at the Austrian Embassy, writes to Grimm a yet more joyous note: "The ball was very lively, for there was a report that everything was definitely agreed. I do not know how it was, for fun or not, but our young lover squeezed the hand of his intended in dancing with her. She turns as pale as death, and tells her governess: 'Just think what he did! He squeezed my hand as we were dancing. I did not know what was going to happen.' 'What did you do then?' 'I was so frightened I nearly dropped.'" After leaving the ball, the young man makes up his mind, and, not wishing to put the affair this time into the hands of the Regent, he goes straight to the Empress, as we have seen.

They are engaged forthwith, and from that moment
are inseparable. They pass their days together under
the mother's eyes, and she continues to recount the
progress of this happiness in which she is so happy to
have some share, now in letters to the grandmother, now
to the absent father, shut up in his gloomy solitude at
Pavlovsk. " My dear good friend, I send you two lines
while our two young people are sitting side by side and
talking in whispers, in which I can only distinguish his
voice. The general (Madame de Lieven), Helen, and I
nous faisons des pâtés, Anne sits on a chair, amusing
herself ; the Regent and Stedingk are by us, looking at
cameos, and I have just told the Regent to go and smoke
on the sofa." She signs this family picture " Masha,"
adding a big kiss for her *mujenok* (little husband). Then
she tells the grandmother how the King has wept at the
thought of leaving his *fiancée* for eight long months, the
marriage having been arranged for the spring. She has
asked him the reason of this long delay. Why should
they not be married at once ? " But the court is not
assembled, and the rooms are not ready." " What
difference does that make ? The court can soon be got
together, and when one is in love, one never notices the
rooms. You can be married, the child can come with
you, and it would be all settled." " But the sea is
dangerous . . ." Here Alexandrine puts in a word :
" I should always feel safe with you." And the mother
adds : " Put your confidence in me, Monsieur Gustave ;
shall I speak to the Empress on your account ?" He
was quite ready, and, adds the excellent princess, " he
was in such high spirits that everybody at supper noticed

it, and he was talking to the child, caressing her even, before everybody."

On the following day there is a fresh note to the father : " My dear good friend, return thanks to God : the betrothal is arranged for Monday evening in the diamond room. . . . It will be done by the metropolitan. . . . Afterwards there will be a ball in the throne-room." Monday evening is the 11th of September. At seven o'clock the persons invited to be present at the ceremony are gathered together in the diamond room. The *fiancée* arrives, then the Empress. Only the young King is missing. He is late in coming, the sovereign begins to show signs of impatience, a quarter of an hour passes, then another quarter of an hour, and Markof enters, trembling and stupefied, and whispers in her ear : " The King will not come ! " She attempts to speak, but not a word leaves her lips ; her *valet de chambre*, Zotof, springs forward with a glass of water ; she drinks a draught, takes a few steps, then raises her hand, and strikes Markof twice with the stick on which she leans in walking ; Bezborodko interposes, but she pushes him aside : " I will teach the brat ! " she is heard to mutter ; then the words choke in her throat, and she drops heavily into a chair.

What has happened ? It has happened that Zubof and Markof, the favourite and his confidant, have set themselves a difficult task without being even aware of its difficulties, and that the Empress has let them act without apparent consciousness that she was confiding her dearest interests to two feather-brains. While the two lovers had exchanged caresses and tender vows, it

had been needful to discuss the conditions of the pro-
jected marriage, and Catherine had demanded from
Gustavus a written agreement that his future wife
should be allowed "entire liberty of conscience and of
worship according to the religion in which she was
born." The prince had replied by referring to the word
of honour he had already given to Her Majesty, "that
the Grand-Duchess should never be interfered with in
her conscience in regard to religion," and by "refusing
to give his signature to any written agreement to this
effect," as being "entirely superfluous." And at the
same time he contrived to attribute to this somewhat
ambiguous word of honour, behind which he intrenched
himself, the weight that he chose to give to it. With
her habitual abruptness and rashness, Catherine had
been a little hasty in judging of this young man whom
she saw for the first time, and in finding in him, from
the very first (as her letters to Grimm prove), "intelligence and goodness of heart, prudence and measure."
He had intelligence, perhaps, but a very singular sort of
intelligence, in which prudence and measure were just
the qualities which never appeared, and his goodness of
heart remained equally problematical. A very pro-
nounced tendency to mystical fanaticism seems to have
always been the most marked trait of his moral phy-
siognomy. Married, later on, to a princess of Baden,
he spent the evening of his wedding-day in reading
the Book of Esther to his wife, and, concerned in
the final coalition against Napoleon, he applied the
prophecies of the Apocalypse to the events which
were then happening. Now, while he is playing, ap-

parently with the utmost sincerity, the part of a fervid
lover, he has been trying to set traps for the poor un-
suspecting girl, by making her take oral engagements,
the sense of which she did not understand. "The fact
is," wrote Catherine to her son after the catastrophe,
"that the King pretended that Alexandrine had promised him to change her religion and take the sacrament in the Lutheran way, and that she had given him
her hand over it. . . . She told me, with the candour
and *naïveté* natural to her, that he had told her that on
the coronation day she would have to take the sacrament with him, and that she had replied : 'Certainly, if
I can, and if grandmamma consents.' And after that he
spoke to her about it again, and she always referred him
to me. I asked her if she had given her hand to the
King by way of promise on this point. At that she
cried with a sort of instinctive fright : 'Never in my
life!'"

A sort of false understanding had thus been created,
which the reassuring declarations showered by Zubof
and his companion on the Empress, in regard to the
state of affairs, had kept up to the very day of the
betrothal. Both sides had counted on the last moment
for carrying everything before them and "patching up"
the ceremony, as Markof expressed it. But, the moment
having come, both parties found themselves at a dead
stand : the signature demanded by the Empress assert-
ing itself on one side, and the pretended engagements
of Paul's daughter, put forward by the prince, on the
other. Zubof had imagined that Gustavus would not
dare to absent himself from the ceremony. He dared,

and Catherine declared next day that the night of the
11th and 12th of July, 1762, when her life and fortune
were at stake, had been less cruel and distressing to her.

II.

She recovers herself, however, immediately, and does
not yet give up hope. The metropolitan of Novgorod,
sent for in such haste, forced to cover two hundred
versts in one day, in order to respond to the sovereign's
appeal, has bowed for hour after hour under the weight
of his priestly vestments and his fatigue ; the assembled
court has yawned till ten o'clock in the evening, waiting
for the great event, and the ball which is to follow :
these are but minor miseries. The energetic sovereign
sets negotiations on foot again at once, and requires her
grand-daughter to be present at another ball, which is to
be given on the occasion of her birthday, and at which
Gustavus is expected to appear. As the poor princess
begs to be allowed to hide her eyes, red this time with
tears not easily dried, she receives a scrap of paper with
these lines : " Why do you weep ? What is put off is
not lost. Wash your eyes with ice and your ears too,
and take Bestujef's drops. Nothing is lost. It is I
who was ill yesterday. You are vexed about the delay :
that is all."

The ball takes place, Alexandra Pavlovna comes, but
the Gustavus that she meets is no longer the amorous
prince ; a militant Lutheran has taken his place. The
rupture is now final. Three years later Alexandra

Pavlovna marries the Archduke Joseph of Austria, and dies soon after (poor frail creature, fated never to taste of happiness) in childbirth. Though she shows no signs of it, Catherine is quite overcome by this trial. Her prestige once compromised, her assurance for the first time impaired, it seems as if the very sources of her life are invaded. She sees a comet, and declares that it is a sign of her approaching end. They remind her that formerly she refused to believe in these super-stitions ; " Yes, formerly ! " she answers sadly. Colics, which she has always suffered from under the stress of violent emotions, now never leave her. Sores break out on her legs. Another adventurer, the famous Lambro-Cazzioni, whom Admiral Ribas has introduced to her, and whose advice she takes as doctor after having em-ployed him as corsair in the Archipelago, recommends her to bathe her feet in iced water. Thereupon she is threatened with congestion and apoplexy. At the beginning of November, however, she feels better. On the 5th of that month, having learnt from a vessel of Lübeck of the retreat of General Moreau across the Rhine, she sends the famous note to Cobenzl : " I hasten to announce to his excellent Excellency that the excel-lent troops of the excellent court have completely beaten the French." That evening at the Hermitage she is very gay, and Leon Naryshkin, who comes in disguised as a street-seller, amuses her greatly. She retires, however, earlier than usual, saying that she has got a colic by laughing so much. Next day she rises at her usual hour, converses for some time with the favour-ite, works with her secretaries, then, dismissing the last one whom she has summoned, she tells him to await her orders in the ante-room. After waiting an unusual time, the man begins to be alarmed. The faithful Zotof ventures, after half-an-hour, to go into the bedroom. The Empress is not there, nor is she in the dressing-room. He sounds an alarm, the attendants hasten in, and after searching everywhere they find her in the closet, rigid, her face convulsed, foaming at the mouth, the death-rattle already in her throat.

A legend states that she had recently placed there a piece of furniture brought from Warsaw among the spoils of Poland : the throne of Poniatowski. It is a vile and filthy idea. Only a " Catherinized Princess of Zerbst," as Joseph called her, could have had such an idea. A daughter of Peter the Great would have remembered that on that throne, before the crowned lover, who had never deserved this deadly insult, other kings had sat, kings who had held the fate of Russia in their mighty hands : Batory, the rude Transylvanian, then Sigismund Vasa, and his son Ladislas. And now the piece of gilded wood, the symbol profaned and degraded by her, avenged itself. It was here that death vanquished the victor.

Carried into her bedroom, stretched on a mattress at the foot of her bed, she agonized for thirty-seven hours without recovering consciousness. When the physicians had declared that there was no more hope, it was observed that Paul was there. Twenty couriers sent by the friends of to-morrow had been sent to seek him at Pavlovsk. A whole *cortège* had welcomed him at the outskirts of the capital. But in the palace, still peopled by the courtiers of Catherine, and where, but a day before, he counted for so little, in the stupefaction in which the unlooked-for catastrophe had cast the whole crowd of men and women, to whom it seems as if the end of the world had come, his presence had not been noticed by any one. An eye-witness, Shishkof, the writer of some curious memoirs, who had come that day to pay court, as usual, to the favourite, gives us in a few expressive strokes an image of the anguish and stupor of this moment. Entering the audience-chamber, he is amazed to find it deserted. Only Lambro-Cazzioni is there, motionless, pale as death, his eyes wide-open and seeing nothing. He answers not a word when spoken to ; he never moves, he looks like a wax figure. Then Nicholas Zubof, one of the brothers of the favourite, appears : he walks like an automaton, and seems to have also lost his tongue. Shishkof decides to beat a retreat. On the staircase he meets Gribovski ; he is about to ask him what has happened ; but he himself becomes voiceless, he cannot get a word out of his lips. He begins to tremble, he knows not why, and his terror increases when he sees that Gribovski also is trembling, and that his lips move without uttering a sound. Each goes his way, without having exchanged a single word. When Shishkof has got out of doors, he begins to run. He returns to his house shivering with fever, and takes to bed without having learnt what has happened.

But Paul does not waste his time. While Rogerson, Zotof, la Pierekussihina, Zubof, press about the dying woman, trying to alleviate her sufferings, wiping away the bloody foam from her lips, he is busy in the next

room with Bezborodko. He searches in the Empress's
writing-desk, and turns over the papers. The general
rumour is that he comes upon a will setting him
aside ; together with an explanatory manifesto, counter-
signed by two popular heroes, Rumiantsof and Suvorof. And the *Pravda voli monarsheï* (law of sovereign
will), established by Peter the Great, remains in force,
by which the monarch has absolute power over the
succession to the throne.

Does Paul really come upon this terrible document at
this moment ? Yes, according to the legend. He discovers an envelope tied with black ribbon, bearing this
inscription : " To be opened after my death, in the
council." Without speaking, he looks at Bezborodko,
who, in equal silence, turns his eyes towards a fire
burning on the hearth, which had been lit, perhaps, only
the other morning, by Catherine herself.

So far the legend ; all that is known to history is that,
a few weeks later, Suvorof is in complete disgrace, and
Rumiantsof, on learning of the death of the great
Empress and the accession of her son, dies suddenly
of an apoplectic fit. Among the papers of Catherine
which are still preserved there is a plan for the settlement of the succession, and Paul is named as heir to
the throne. But it is of early date, contemporary, in
all probability, with the legislative commission (1767).

The accession of Paul is effected without difficulty,
and, outside the court, the effect produced by the death
of her into whose heritage he enters is far from corresponding with the impression so eloquently rendered by
Shishkof. Langeron notes in his memoirs : " When I

received the official information, I made my regiment, as I was ordered, take oath of allegiance to the Emperor Paul. I was astonished by the indifference with which the soldiers and officers of the army received the news. They showed neither sorrow nor regret." We have already observed, that though Catherine took victory on pay, according to a courtly French volunteer, and in spite of the military air of her whole reign, she was not popular with the army, and the Russian people as a whole were some time in realizing that, with her, it buried a past glory which was not soon to live again. Europe at that moment had no time to think of what was happening at St. Petersburg : the very day when the Empress heaved her last sigh, with the consoling vision of the triumph of the coalition over the revolutionary armies, a general other than Moreau crossed the bridge of Arcola in a storm of enthusiasm, which prophesied of Austerlitz.

III.

The gratitude of Russia was slow in manifesting itself, even in the erection of a monument worthy of the modern Semiramis. Catherine, indeed, while she was living, had refused to receive any such honours. " I will not have a monument," she wrote to Grimm, September 20, 1783, " and if the divine (Reiffenstein) dreams of one, I do not grudge him the pleasure, but it shall never be carried out with my consent. The squares at St. Petersburg are already crowded." She discouraged statues, and professed to tolerate caricatures ; she was the first to laugh over them, sometimes a rather forced laugh, as in another letter to the "fag": " In Holland they have made a medal, where the Queen-Empress and the Empress of Russia are sitting together in a chariot, and the King of Prussia is on the driver's seat. They are asked where they are going, and they reply : ' Where the driver likes to take us.' It seemed to me very amusing. It only lacks truth or the music of a French comic opera, the former to be piquant, the latter to be an absolute platitude." Sometimes, indeed, she was moved to anger, and caused certain designs, whose licence and obscenity justly seemed to her to pass all bounds, to be burnt by the hangman. A great quantity of them are to be seen in contemporary collections : for the most part they defy description, like that " Supper of Catherine," the inscription on which may be thus paraphrased : " Since you are so fond of men, eat their flesh and drink their blood ;" or like that other, which represents the Empress with one foot on Warsaw, the other on Constantinople, covering with her vast skirts all the princes of Europe, the Pope included. But doubtless she imagined that after her death some Falconet, perhaps some Russian Falconet, would do for her what she had done for Peter the Great. Employed to paint the portrait for the capitulary hall of the Order of St. George, Lampi placed a bust of the great Tsar in the background of his canvas, with this inscription : " What he began, she accomplished."

Falconet was late in coming. In 1848, some poor German refugees settled at Saratof took the first

step, by setting on a modest pedestal the figure of
the sovereign to whom their fathers owed so much.
The gratitude of the direct heirs of a glory which
filled Europe for a quarter of a century was only
expressed in 1883, and then only by the erection
of a monument which is more pompous and less
happy. Set up in St. Petersburg, in the middle of a
vast square which stretches between the Imperial
Library, the Anitchkof Palace, the present abode of
the Tsar, and the Alexander Theatre, M. Mikieshin's
work is somewhat unattractive in aspect. With her
attitude, which is that of a person walking, and her
sceptre in her hand, the Empress looks as if she were
following a procession, carrying a candle. The plinth
of the column, which is done in imitation of the monument of Frederick at Berlin, is an attempt to do in
bronze something like what we have attempted to do
here. The principal figures in the Empress's *entourage*
are there: Patiomkin, with one foot on the Turkish
turban ; Orlof, the conqueror of Tchesmé, and Rumiantsof the conqueror of Kagoul, the Princess Dashkof,
Betzki, and Dierjavin. But the bronze has done injustice to the artist's conception, the figures are awkward
and uncouth, the conqueror of the Crimea looks ill
rather than triumphant, the fierce *Balafré* seems to be
doing penance. The *ensemble* of the monument calls
up the notion of those little bells that used to be seen on
every table, a Napoleon with folded arms for a handle.

Bronze and marble have alike done injustice to the
memory of Catherine. Printing ink has done her
better service : the sole monument worthy of her up to

the present is that which the publications of the Imperial Historical Society of Russia have raised to her. But this is but a collection of materials. "Happy the writer of the future who shall write the life of Catherine II.," said Voltaire. I do not pretend to this good fortune : I have but endeavoured to open up a path, in which I am certain that others will come after me.

THE END.